◇◇◇◇◇◇◇◇◇◇◇

Shanjamo Jungi

THE FIRST NAGA EDUCATED
IN THE UNITED STATES OF AMERICA
1882–1956

SECOND EDITION

Shanjamo Jungi

A BIOGRAPHY BY JAN EZUNG NIENU

Dorylus Publishing Group

ISBN-13: 9798648072046
Publication Date: June 2020
Dorylus Publishing Group
Second Edition

Cover design, interior design, and composition:
Leigh McLellan Design

◇◇◇◇◇◇◇◇◇◇◇

Dedication

This book is dedicated to:

The American Baptist Missionaries who brought
the Gospel of Jesus Christ to Nagaland.

The first Naga converts and the early church planters of Nagaland.

Because of your sacrifices, we have the gift of salvation
through Jesus Christ.

*Blessed are those who are persecuted because of righteousness,
for theirs is the kingdom of heaven.*

*Blessed are you when people insult you, persecute you
and falsely say all kinds of evil against you because of me.*

*Rejoice and be glad, because great is your reward in heaven,
for in the same way they persecuted the prophets who were before you.*

Matthew 5:10–12, NIV

Contents

Foreword
Peter Weis, Archivist Northfield Mount Hermon, ix

Acknowledgments, xi

Introduction, 1

The Early Years, 5

American Baptist Mission, 9

Chapter 22: Prædicans ad Confluentes, 21

Chapter 23: Sing Praises, 25

West Trenton, 27

Rev. Samuel Alden Perrine, B.S., B.Th.,
and Rose Ermina Lamb Perrine, 31

Northfield Mount Hermon School, 37

Dr. Henry Franklin Cutler, 43

Shanjamo's Ministry in the Naga Hills, 51

Shanjamo's Family Life, 71

Shanjamo Memorial Baptist High School, 77

A Collection of Letters and Forms, 79

A Tribute, 119

References, 121

About the Author, 123

Peter H. Weis, Archivist,
Northfield Mount Hermon School, Massachusets USA

◇◇◇◇◇◇◇◇◇◇

Foreword

May 15, 2019

I N 1905, A young man arrived in the United States from his home in Nagaland, a remote state in the mountainous northeast corner of India. He came under the wing of a missionary couple returning to Port Norris, New Jersey, on furlough and studied there for two years. He showed great promise in that time, both as a scholar and as having formed a singular purpose in life: to become an educator among his compatriots in the Naga Hills. Those around him in Port Norris were impressed enough by Lomongo Sanjamo's devotion to this goal that they conceived to support his admission and attendance at Mount Hermon School. Located in a remote valley in western Massachusetts, it perhaps sometimes seemed to him at least as remote as his home in Yikhum. He studied there for three terms before returning to his home in Nagaland. Armed with this education and full of the inspiration it also engendered, he began his career in teaching and Christian missionary work. Years later, he recalled Mount Hermon as a place that had nurtured his soul. As the archivist at Northfield Mount Hermon, the school which Sanchamo attended more than a century ago, I've been delighted to share with Jan Ezung Nienu a small but important corner of a great man's life. What follows is his whole story.

Peter H. Weis
Archivist
Northfield Mount Hermon, Massachusetts, USA

◇◇◇◇◇◇◇◇◇◇

Acknowledgments

M Y GRATITUDE IS extended to Elder (*Eramo*) Wosumo Kikon of Yikhum Village who was 103 years young when I interviewed him. He was a neighbor of the late Evangelist Shanjamo. I am also grateful to Elder (*Eramo*) Yantsao Jungi, 81 years young, and Elder (*Eramo*) Ngheo Jungi, 93 years young at the time of the interview. These three gentlemen gave me many insights into the life of Shanjamo. They were interviewed together in June of 2016 at Yikhum Village, Nagaland.

Appreciation belongs to the relatives of Shanjamo, for overseeing this research project for accuracy, and to Mr. Yanrenthung, Shanjamo's only living adopted son, who gave me firsthand information about the kind, accepting, caring, loving, giving, and forgiving father he knew, who showed and taught him the love of Jesus. Shanjamo tirelessly shared and preached the gospel of Jesus Christ until he went home to be with the Lord.

My heartfelt gratitude to Mr. and Mrs. Mhabemo Jungi for welcoming me to their home and serving me freshly plucked cucumbers, fresh corn, and amazing Lotha cuisine—a warm Naga hospitality I will not forget. The Yikhum Village cucumbers are the best-tasting cucumbers, soft and not crunchy, so delicious, and very sweet. I thank you for your time and the information given for the completion of this project.

During my visit to Nagaland in July of 2019 for the final approval and consultation of the biography, Mr. Mhabemo Jungi accompanied me to Changsu Village, where Evangelist Shanjamo pastored many years ago. I am very grateful to him for his assistance as our tour guide. I was very impressed with Yikhum Village, Riphym Village, and Changsu Village. The villages were extremely clean with absolutely no litter. Changsu Village had a trash can beside the road on every corner. I was so impressed to learn that Yikhum Village is an alcohol, tobacco and drug-free zone. A sign is posted indicating that whoever is caught drinking, doing drugs, or smoking will be fined heavily.

All of these factors reveal a sincere ownership of their environment. This is a great lesson for us to learn: to protect, care for, preserve, respect, and show deep appreciation for our habitat. Everyone we met at the villages was extremely welcoming. An elderly lady from Changsu Village saw us, and although we were strangers, she invited us to her home for tea. We graciously declined as we needed to drive to where we were staying before the rain started pouring again. Her hospitality was admirable.

The elders and the relatives of Shanjamo lifted me up to the Lord in prayers for blessings and guidance from above as I embarked on this project to shed some light on the contributions of Evangelist Shanjamo. Every time we got together for consultations, prayers were offered to heaven. My heart is blessed and filled with joy at the sweet memories of these times together.

Mr. Azo Nienu, current member of Nagaland Legislative Assembly and former minister of Nagaland Government, loaned me his vehicle as I travelled between villages. The roads were treacherous, filled with giant potholes. Because the roads were not paved, travelling in the monsoon rain was a challenge. The few areas that were paved at one time have been washed away by the rain due to poor workmanship. Our driver, Vikas, did a fantastic job navigating the windy, slippery roads of Nagaland.

A heartfelt gratitude is extended to Ken and LaDawn Wilford for making it possible for my husband and me to visit Port Norris Baptist Church, New Jersey, and for taking us around Port Norris.

To Mr. Peter H. Weis, archivist of Mt. Hermon School, sincere thanks for his valuable time and generosity in sharing information about the prestigious school Shanjamo Lomongo attended, dedication in sharing the carefully archived letters, and permission to use some of the incredible old pictures of Northfield Mount Hermon. I am thankful for his support for the completion of this biography and for his willingness to write the foreword for this book.

I am thankful to my husband Dr. Vic Nienu for reviewing the text in its entirety and giving me helpful comments and suggestions. He travelled with me to Port Norris, New Jersey, and Northfield Mount Hermon, Massachusetts, to visit the institutions where Shanjamo Lomongo Jungi studied.

It was a joyful, as well as emotional, journey for us as we visited the places Shanjamo had lived and frequented. We stayed at Melville, New Jersey, where he visited often. It was a joy for us to visit Morristown, New Jersey, where his sponsors resided, and Greenfield, Massachusetts, a beautiful city where he visited his optometrist. While we stayed at Greenfield, we drove around Brattleboro, where his osteopath practiced.

During our travel, our conversations centered around our amazement at the young Shanjamo, a native of the Naga Hills who had studied there over 100 years ago. We both consider him to have been extraordinarily adventurous and brave to leave his homeland. We also have a deep admiration for his family in the Naga Hills for allowing him to leave his homeland to study abroad. In the early days, it was out of character for a Naga family to send their children away to study since the Naga community is close-knit and prefers to habitat together. Being chosen by Dr. Clark also showed the tremendous trust and confidence placed in Shanjamo. We also admire the wonderful love and friendship shared between Shanjamo and the Perrines.

Notes to the Second Edition

Right after I released the first edition of the biography, I was in Calcutta Nagaland House with my nieces Elilo and Dorothy. Through

Google, Dorothy found the book Mark W. Falzini wrote where he mentioned Shanjamo in one of his chapters. As soon as I landed in San Francisco, I ordered all his books. I read his book, *One Square Mile*, where he mentioned Young Shanjamo coming to Trenton Junction, living with the Lambs (parents of Mrs. Perrine), and attending Trenton Junction Public School. I was blown away to discover this missing link, much needed information to complete the itinerary of Shanajmo Jungi's biography.

I wasted no time in trying to connect with Mark through his publisher. At the same time, Dorothy reached out to Mark via Facebook and that is how we got connected. Mark graciously welcomed me to West Trenton. Connecting with Mark W. Falzini is like finding Nemo. I was extremely fortunate to have found the needle in the haystack. Thank you Mark for saving me hours of research and taking me straight to the source. The connection between West Trenton and Nagaland is solid and binding with the rich history we share.

Mark provided the missing chapter which led to the second edition of this book, thus completing the itinerary of Shanjamo Jungi's stay in the United States. My intention in his biography is not to go after or expose the wrongdoings of others done to him. Shanjamo Jungi as a godly man and a forgiving person would have wanted the power of forgiveness to resonate like a trumpet sound. This biography is to celebrate his accomplishments and provide documentation of his itinerary and schools attended in the United States which is long overdue. A few minor changes were also made, including the picture of the home where he lived, the school he attended, and the church where he preached during his stay at West Trenton, formerly known as Trenton Junction.

Mark W. Falzini gave me permission to include Chapter 22 and 23 from his book since it narrates the arrival of a young Naga boy by the name of Shanjamo Jungi to West Trenton.

Mark W. Falzini wrote the following books: *One Square Mile, Letters Home, The Siege of Jutland, Their Fifteen Minutes, Biographical Sketches of the Lindberg Case, Lindberg Kidnapping* and was my source leading to the second edition. Mark is a local historian and archivist for the New Jersey State Police Museum. He is an internationally known expert on the Lindberg kidnapping case. He is also a life-long resident of West Trenton. Through Mark, I discovered that Junction Trenton had changed its name to West Trenton.

To my colleague Taiko Roskothen who jumped on the plane with me to New Jersey on short notice. Thank you for your support throughout our adventure. We discovered an amazing tasty pork roll in New Jersey. It was so delicious that we brought home a few logs of pork roll and shared it with friends and family. Their reviews were excellent as we expected.

The Houstons served as the last missionaries to the Lotha Naga Tribe. Before Mrs. Harriet Houston passed away, she gave us slides taken in Nagaland during their stay in the Naga Hills from 1947–1953. Mrs. Houston also gave us their letters and other valuable documents. Recently, as my husband sorted the slides taken by Mrs. Houston, he came across clearly labelled pictures of Shanjamo Jungi. This find was truly a real treasure. Shanjamo's picture on the cover of the first edition was a copy, as was indicated. I am thrilled to have discovered these pictures taken by the Houstons. The pictures are clear, and the medals he earned as a war veteran are clearly shown with distinct colors. I am very happy to include these pictures in the second edition.

My sincere heartfelt gratitude to my sister Mrs. Abeni TCK Lotha for providing me with many resources and for her valuable feedback. Thank you for being my mentor and for your constant encouragement and prayers. After our parents went home to be with the Lord, my sister took over their role, guiding us and supporting us emotionally and spiritually.

For the friendship, wisdom, guidance, love, and kindness of the many wonderful people whom God has blessed me with, I am thankful, grateful, and so blessed to have you in my life. There are more good people on this earth than those very few bad people.

◇◇◇◇◇◇◇◇◇◇

Introduction

G ROWING UP IN Nagaland, I often heard from my parents, teachers, and church leaders about the missionaries who brought the gospel of Jesus Christ to the Naga Hills. Especially I remember my Dad's recounting the story of evangelist, pastor, First World War veteran, and teacher Shanjamo Jungi. Although I was a young girl at the time, I was intrigued by the story of this man and about the lifestyles and cultures of different lands. My dad purchased many books from traveling businessmen who came to sell their merchandise. I adored books and enthusiastically read whatever literature my dad brought home.

I decided to write Shanjamo's biography because I was fascinated by this incredible man's life, his journey, and his contribution to the early Naga churches. As a Lotha Naga myself, now living in the United States, my desire was to document his experiences as a student both in the US and in his homeland as a missionary of God. Shanjamo could have chosen to settle in the United States after his studies, but instead he was led by the Holy Spirit to evangelize the Nagas with the gospel of Jesus Christ. It is a great privilege for me to tell the story of Evangelist Shanjamo Jungi, and I thank the Lord for leading me to honor him with the completion of his biography. I have a great deal of respect for him, considering he gave so much to improve the lives of the Nagas through his leadership and commitment to evangelism.

The missionaries addressed him as *Sanchamo,* as evidenced by their letters. His Lotha given name is Shanchamo; his tombstone is inscribed as *Shanjamo.* All documents from his village, Yikhum, addressed him as either *Shanjamo* or *Shanchamo.* Also, a school is named after him using *Shanchamo.* He himself always spelled his name as *Sanchamo,* as seen from all of his correspondence, reproduced here. For the title of this book, as well as for readability throughout, the name Shanjamo is used.

According to Yikhum Baptist Church, Shanjamo was born in 1882. Mrs. Perrine, who filled out the Mount Hermon application form for Shanjamo, indicated that he was born about 1887. During those days, there were no hospitals; therefore, childbirth took place at home, assisted by the elderly women in the village. Birth certificates were unheard of, making it difficult to document accurate birth dates.

Evangelist Shanjamo, the American Baptist missionaries, and the early pioneer Christians who served in Nagaland left behind a great example for us to emulate. Reading this book will strengthen your faith and bless your heart. Within its pages, you will find examples of fortitude to help you meet the challenges of today; encouragement to use your time wisely, show human kindness, and make a positive difference wherever you are; and a reminder that we did not come to this world to live forever. Our time on earth is short and fleeting. Everywhere I turn, I find that many people I know and love have either passed on or are struggling with health issues. I find myself buying more sympathy cards as the years go by.

The Naga people have freedom of worship because of the sacrifices made by our early church planters. Many people in this world cannot worship openly, and underground churches still exist around the world. The Nagas are blessed to have the freedom to worship Jesus Christ without any restrictions.

This biographical sketch, though brief, will show you the power of love and forgiveness through Christ. Evangelist Shanjamo and the early Christians were ridiculed by many, but they forgave and continued to preach the love of Jesus.

Let us respect and lift up the servants of the Lord everywhere as they work tirelessly in obedience to the Holy Spirit to bring peace, preach the gospel, and help make this world a better place to live for a short time on this earth.

My deepest gratitude goes to the American Baptist missionaries and to the early Naga converts who sacrificed their lives so that the Naga people today may have the gift of salvation. Because of the coming of Christianity, head hunting practices came to an end in Nagaland. In the profound words of the late Mr. Imlong Chang, a pioneer among the Chang Naga Tribe, "Our people have been greatly blessed by the coming of Christianity. How good it is that it is now possible for the head and the body to be buried together."

I was unable to locate any of Shanjamo's pictures, either from Nagaland or from Northfield Mount Hermon. The picture used in this book is copied from the cover of *Memories of His Educational Journey to America*, published by Yikhum Baptist Church. By looking at his picture, we can conclude that he was a handsomely built man, well decorated with medals of honor, and a truly dignified and accomplished individual.

Our past presents many possibilities that shape our future. Our history allows appreciation, as well as the process of elimination to change for the better, thus making a positive paradigm shift for the community and the world in which we live.

We must not forget our rich Christian heritage and the sacrifices made by the early Christians for our freedom today. May the Lord bless you and fill your heart with gratitude and the desire to do good deeds and make this world a better place as you read the biography of pastor, evangelist, First World War veteran and teacher, Shanjamo Lomongo Jungi Lotha

Although I tried my best to document and report accurate information, I apologize for any discrepancies. The intent of this biography is to honor this great man who was anointed by the Holy Spirt to preach the gospel. All glory and honor belongs to our Lord and Savior Jesus Christ.

This manuscript is written in modern American English. Unless otherwise noted, the original documents are retained as written without any corrections, including any spelling discrepancies where they exist.

◇◇◇◇◇◇◇◇◇◇

The Early Years

CCORDING TO THE Yikhum Baptist Centennial Book, Shanjamo was born on January 2, 1882, at Yikhum Village, an hour's drive from Wokha. He was born into the Lotha Naga Tribe of Nagaland. He also had an older brother. Shanjamo's mother died when he was a young boy, so Shanjamo went to stay with his uncle. When Shanjamo turned 16 years old in 1898, Elder Nkhao Jungi took him to Impur to seek a better education at Dr. Clark's school. Here he studied from 1898 to 1904 and successfully passed class 5 (fifth grade). Shanjamo was baptized by Rev. W.F. Dowd on January 4, 1899, and subsequently became a member of the Impur Baptist Church.

Dr. Edward Winter Clark immediately recognized Shanjamo's potential to further the kingdom of God and continue the work that had already been entrusted by the American Baptist missionaries among the Nagas in the Naga Hills. Dr. Clark took great interest in Shanjamo, a gifted student, and therefore recommended that Rev. and Mrs. Perrine take him to the United States to further his education. It appears that Dr. Clark was a planner, a far-sighted man who clearly saw the need for the continuation of the ministry, and as a result, he chose Shanjamo to be fully equipped by educating him in the States for future ministry.

Dr. Edward Winter Clark and his wife Mary Mead Clark, the first American Baptist missionaries to the Naga Hills, discovered Shanjamo at the Impur School, which Dr. Clark had established. Because of Shanjamo's competence and proficiency in the English language, he was chosen from among many students and given the opportunity to study in the United States with the purpose of returning to the Naga Hills to carry on the ministry. Shanjamo stood out from among his peers as a capable and contributing citizen. He was social, outgoing, and fiercely independent, traits Americans embrace in a personality.

At the Okotso Baptist Church centennial jubilee celebration (2004), it was reported that Evangelists Shanjamo and Shanrio went to Okotso Village in 1901 and preached the good news of Jesus Christ. The villagers looked down upon them, ignored them and even laughed at their preaching. There were no converts at this time at Okotso Village. However, there was a young man by the name Etssisao who was listening and paying attention to their message. As a result of their ministry, Etssisao later accepted Christ as his Savior. Eventually, he went to Impur to study the Word of God. After completing his studies in 1904, Mr. Etssisao returned and became the first pastor of his village at Okotso Baptist Church.

Documentation indicates (Murry 1979:35) that during the sixth session of the American Baptist Missionary Union, December 22–31, 1900, Rev. S.A. Rivenburg reported the following:

> There is one very hopeful feature of the work for the Lothas. For several years there have been Lotha boys in the Impur School. This year there were six. Five of whom have been baptized. Of these five, one is likely to prove a good preacher. He is now away among his own people preaching, but will return to the Impur School for another year.

Dr. Sidney White Rivenburg, M.D., and his wife, Hattie Elizabeth Tiffany Rivenburg, served as missionaries to the Ao Naga Tribe and the Angami Naga Tribe. They preached and practiced medicine among the Nagas. Mrs. Hattie Rivenburg died in Kohima on March

22, 1908 (Nagaland Baptist Church Council 2012:56). She died after a surgical procedure, leaving behind their little daughter Narola. Their daughter, Dr. Narola Rivenburg, Ph.D., later served as a missionary to the Ao Naga Tribe. She was born in Kohima on November 17, 1887, and was also baptized in Kohima in 1895. On December 28, 1910, in Nowgong, Assam, Dr. Rivenburg re-married Helen B. Protzman, who was also serving as a missionary under the Women's Society of Nowgong. In the year 1922, Dr. Rivenburg was honored by the British government and awarded the prestigious Kaiser-i-Hind medal for his outstanding work among the Nagas.

I have no doubt in my mind that the young man mentioned by Rev. Rivenburg was Shanjamo, who apparently was a gifted preacher and, as a result, was given the opportunity to receive further education in the United States.

Dr. Clark entrusted the Perrines to take with them this young, outstanding Lotha Naga boy to be educated in the United States. Upon their return from the Naga Hills as missionaries, the Perrines pastored at the First Baptist Church in Port Norris, New Jersey. This is where Shanjamo attended the Port Norris Public School. Later the Perrines arranged for Shanjamo to attend Northfield Mount Hermon School in Massachusetts. After the completion of his studies, he returned to his homeland and preached the Word of God passionately.

Rev. and Mrs. S.A. Perrine (1892–1905) took Shanjamo into their care and lovingly referred to him as their own child, bringing him to the United States to be educated. According to a letter from Mrs. Perrine, Shanjamo came to the United States in 1904, Mrs. Perrine also documented that Shanjamo understood and spoke the English language well. The many letters penned by the Perrines indicated their love for the Naga people and their desire to educate Shanjamo so that he could go back and teach the Naga people the gospel of Jesus Christ.

In a letter to Professor Henry Cutler, the principal of Mount Hermon School, Rev. Samuel Perrine advised him to continue to refer to their new student by his given name, *Sanchamo*, and not to give or call him by any other name.

Shanjamo's public school teacher, Miss Elda G. Stambaugh, gave a recommendation of Shanjamo, adding, "He is somewhat closed and at times finds difficulty expressing himself." She praised him as someone who was honest, conscientious, and easy to discipline.

Shanjamo never took for granted the opportunity to study in the United States. He was very thankful to the Perrines and to Mrs. Ropes, who sponsored him to attend Mount Hermon School. As a follower of Jesus Christ, he embraced the plan of salvation, and his desire was to go back and evangelize the Naga people after his studies.

Shanjamo appeared to be a very patient and tolerant man. He was also someone who was adventurous, open-minded, and eager to learn. Shanjamo was ahead of his time, continuously expanding his horizons by embracing new experiences.

The biography of Shanjamo Jungi is an incredible story of courage, love, forgiveness, endurance, and sacrifice. This is a story about a man who embraced and lived between two cultures and who persevered through the challenges of both American and Naga culture. Shanjamo exhibited and modeled what it is to be a follower of Jesus Christ, to love one another, forgive one another, and share the gospel of Christ. This is a story about a young man who was chosen from among many students and given the opportunity to study in the United States in the early 1900's, the first Naga to be educated in such a prestigious institution. Like the rest of us, Evangelist Shanjamo was certainly not a perfect man, but the contributions he made were truly admirable. During his early life, education and Christianity were mostly unheard of, as many of the Nagas were still practicing a primitive way of life.

American Baptist Mission

I T IS VALUABLE to understand the work of the American Baptist missionaries, both men and women, who gave up the comforts of home to serve the Lord overseas to introduce the salvation of Jesus. These early missionaries showed great foresight as they invested in the future of the Naga people by ensuring that Shanjamo was prepared to teach his own people. Nagas were known for their fearless head-hunting practices before the gospel was brought to Nagaland, and the missionaries were clearly aware of the risks involved when entering the Naga Hills. The American Baptist missionaries were some of the first outsiders to encounter these head-hunting warrior tribes call the Nagas.

From 1838 to 1841, Rev. Miles Bronson started his mission work among the Singphos in Assam and the Konyak Naga Tribe. He was the first missionary to enter the then Naga Hills, reaching out to the Konyak Tribe. He started a school at Namsang in the Konyak area. Due to lack of proper food and accommodations, as well as other inconveniences, his work with the Nagas was suspended (M.M. Clark 1907:5).

Mrs. Mary Mead Clark, wife of missionary Dr. Clark, writes, "From the broad verandah of the mission bungalow, we looked out day after day, on and on beyond the villages, across the rice fields, over the jungles of the plains, upon the mountains towering in silent grandeur against the southern sky, as if watching for the feet of him who bringeth good tidings that publisheth peace" (M.M. Clark 1907:9). She documented that "My soul is not at rest: there comes a strange and secret whisper to my spirit."

God was leading the Clarks to share the gospel of Jesus Christ to the Nagas in the Naga Hills. The Clarks told the Assamese Christians about their desire to minister to the Nagas in the Naga Hills. The Assamese Christians continued to warn the Clarks about the warring Nagas who went from village to village taking heads. Mrs. Clark recorded that Dr. Clark responded by saying,

"The voice of my departed Lord,
'Go teach all nations,'
Comes on the night air and awakes my ear,
And I will go" (M.M. Clark 1907:11).

Later in 1871, an Assamese evangelist by the name of Godhula befriended Mr. Supongmeren, an Ao Naga living in Sibsagar, Assam. Mr. Supongmeren taught Evangelist Godhula and Dr. Clark the Ao dialect and Naga customs. Soon Godhula, with the help of Mr. Supongmeren, learned about the Naga people and decided to head up to the hills to Molongkimong Village in order to share the gospel of Jesus Christ. (Nagaland Baptist Church Council 1912:176).

At first Godhula was kept as a prisoner in the village and guarded by the tribesmen. According to Mrs. Clark, "Godhula, in his deep-toned, melodious voice, poured out his soul in sweet gospel hymns. The people flocked around him and listened as he told them in his own eloquent way, the sweet old, old story." (Clark 1907:11). The Nagas love to sing, and music helped to open the lines of communication. No longer a prisoner, Godhula was embraced by the Naga tribes, and those who had once been his captors now accepted him as one of their own.

The village people, women and children wept in sorrow when Evangelist Godhula decided to return to Sibsagar. He was given the proper honor of an escort of forty men to accompany him to the door of the mission bungalow in Sibsagar. "These men seated on our veranda were picturesque and an interesting sight, and far-reaching and full of meaning was our conference with them concerning future visits." (Clark 1907:12).

Even in the midst of their head-hunting and primitive living, the Nagas embraced and loved music. They sang in the form of chanting melodious tunes. They sang while working in the field, during ceremonial events, and in their everyday living. Music is a universal language that has no boundaries, bringing joy and peace. We have experienced that music brings healing to our soul and tears of joy or sadness to our eyes. Music brings smiles to our faces, melts our hearts, and makes us reflect on many things. Music brings us into the presence of the Lord. To this day, the Nagas enjoy singing, and music is an integral part in the lives of the Nagas.

Every culture celebrates its own beautiful music. Music is a sustaining force. For the Nagas, the love for music is embedded in their souls. Understanding the Nagas' love of music, God used the gifted baritone voice of Evangelist Godhula to draw attention and unite their spirits, leading to friendship and acceptance of the gospel. Music broke down the barrier of suspicion between the Nagas and the stranger in their land. Music brought light into the darkness.

A careful reading of well-preserved documents makes it evident that the Nagas, although fierce and warlike, were also caring, loving, and hospitable. Even to this day, the Nagas are known for their warmth, hospitality, and love of music.

Evangelist Godhula was one of the first pioneers to preach the gospel of Jesus Christ to the then primitive Naga tribes. He was instrumental in paving the way for Dr. Clark and his wife Mary Mead Clark, as well as for the rest of the American Baptist missionaries who followed in their footsteps to Nagaland.

Mary Mead Clark made the following observation:

In April 1872, Godhula and his wife Lucy, a former pupil of Mrs. Whiting's school, started for the hills to remain through the rains. This was a bold venture. No one from civilization had before attempted it. On account of the difficulty of communication with the plains in the wet season, we seldom heard from them, but they were held before the throne in many prayers by the missionaries and the Christians in Sibsagar (M.M. Clark: 1907:12).

It is hard to fathom the joy, as well as the trepidation, that Godhula and Lucy must have felt as they prayerfully took the brave step to climb the Naga Hills to share the gospel of Jesus Christ. Many prayers were sent daily for the safety of the traveling missionaries, and in the end all were answered. Mrs. Clark documented, "No one from civilization has attempted to go to the Naga Hills for fear that they will not come back alive."

As a Naga myself and a follower of Jesus Christ, I am thankful to Dr. Clark, Mary Mead Clark, and the rest of the American Baptist missionaries who gave up their positions in America and sacrificed comfort and familiarity for the sake of the gospel. They were separated from their loved ones and missed many milestones like birthdays and anniversaries. One can only imagine their dedication and desire to spread the gospel of Jesus Christ.

Evangelist Godhula had come to know Christ through the American Baptist missionaries. He then risked his own life and traveled to the Naga Hills to further the teachings of the gospel. Dr. Clark followed and set up the mission center at Impur. Mary Mead Clark gave a touching account that "these wild men, battle-axe and spear in hand, with stammering tongues, tried to tell in broken Assamese, with the help in as imperfect Naga from their teacher, of this newly found Saviour and of their desire to follow in his ordinances" (M.M.Clark 1907:13).

According to a letter written by Mrs. Clark on August 24, 1904, their missionary endeavor was a daring one: "We labored for the Assamese until becoming interested in the uncivilized warlike Hill Tribes in the South of Assam, where no one had carried the blessed gospel.

My husband entered upon this work beyond British rule, with no protection from English government, and I joined him in 1878 after a visit in America."

Mrs. Clark eloquently described their trails to the Naga Hills as passing by feathery, waving bamboos, intertwined and interlaced, and fantastic arbors with orchids swaying in the mountain breeze. Their trails took them up the hills, down the lower hills, around the streams, and through the majestic mountains of the Naga Hills. One can only imagine their joy mixed with tremendous anxiety as they climbed to reach their destination. Mrs. Clark documented that "my attention was directed to a precipitous descent on the left of our path, where not long before, a party ambushing just above swooped down upon some travelers, leaving 25 bodies headless." (M.M. Clark 1907:31). Their hearts must have jumped at seeing such sight, yet they continued their journey to answer the call of God, never wavering in their faith.

Mrs. Clark writes in a letter on August 24,1904, "These Naga tribes were without a written language not a letter even. Mr. Clark using the Roman character reduced the language to writing when school books, hymns books and scripture translations followed."

As a result of their newfound hope in Jesus Christ, the Ao Nagas readily and joyfully welcomed Dr. Clark to the Naga Hills. Rev. Bengt and Edna Anderson, who served as missionaries to the Sema Naga Tribe from 1936–1948, documented that the Ao Tribe had been fortunate in being the first to welcome missionaries and to work with them, and they continued to be favored by having more missionaries than any of the rest of the tribes (Anderson 1978:38).

The American Baptist missionaries entered the Naga Hills again in 1872 to evangelize the head-hunting tribes of the Nagas. Dr. Clark was the first missionary to encounter the Ao Naga Tribe. In addition to the mission at Impur, he also set up a school to educate the young Nagas. It was not an easy task for the Clarks to start from scratch, but they did so with the help of the Naga believers and the power of the Holy Spirit.

Their house was built with *okshi* (palm) leaves for the roof and split-plaited bamboo tied together with rattans for doors. It included two rooms and a storehouse. Mrs. Clark described their home in the following words,

You see, we do not care to put on any style here, but we are glad to be able to live happily and cozily and contentedly amid our surroundings, so different and with resources so much less than we had in America. Our house has three rooms and a store room, is built of rough-hewn posts, roof covered with grass, the side walls with two thicknesses of bamboo mats, the inner one finer and lighter than the outer. They are both woven by the Nagas, and afford only a partial protection from the cold (M.M. Clark 1907:134).

They lived among the primitive Nagas, wild elephants, boars, and tigers. In what must have been a harrowing experience, Mrs. Clark reported that one night several tigers ate some of their livestock. She also documented concerning the flora:

Orchids, rhododendrons, beautifully colored begonias, tree fern, ground fern, mosses and creepers in great variety and luxuriance. Flowers such as hollyhock, elder, gentian, morning glory, lady slipper, blue bell, English violet, lilies and other homeland flowers were found beneath the welcome shade of the familiar oak, walnut, or other well-known trees. Fruit such as mangoes, oranges, limes, bananas, figs, crab apples, cherries, raspberries, strawberries and others were also grown. Crops such as rice, yams, tobacco, ginger, red peppers, betel were also grown" (M.M. Clark 1907:37).

In 1885, Mrs. Clark happily reported that 51 Nagas and 3 Assamese had been baptized in the Ao Naga mission. After sixteen years on the mission field in Assam and the Naga Hills, the Clarks took their first furlough in 1885, then returned to the Naga Hills in 1886.

According to Rev. Dowd, in 1905 there were 191 baptisms recorded, and in 1906, 138 baptisms were added. Finally, in 1906 a membership totaling 760 Christians was reported. God was at work, and Christianity was growing in the Naga Hills. Dr. Clark and Mary Mead Clark must have rejoiced, giving praises to the Lord for having seen souls won over from the awful and terrifying practices of head-hunting. The Clarks, Evangelist Godhula, and Lucy saw their hard work pay off. Our Heavenly Father continues to bless the work that originated with Evangelist Godhula and his wife Lucy, Dr. and Mrs. Clark, and the other missionaries who served in the Naga Hills. Because of their selfless sacrifices, today there are churches in every village, town, and city in Nagaland.

Shanjamo was a student of Dr. and Mrs. Clark at Impur, where the Baptist missionaries received orientation before being sent on deputation to the various tribes of Nagaland. Rev. and Mrs. Bengt Anderson were sent to evangelize the Sema Naga Tribe in the district of Zunheboto. Dr. Witter and Mary Potter went to the Lotha Tribe. Later Rev. Howard and Harriet Houston lived at Vankhosung Mission Center with the Lotha Tribe, where they served and evangelized the Lothas in the Wokha District. Rev. King and Dr. Rivenburg served the Angami Tribe in the Kohima district. In the book *Billy Graham, Evangelist to the World: An Authorized Biography of the Decisive Years*, author John Pollock quotes Billy Graham as saying that "American Baptist missionaries entered to evangelize the Ao Tribe in 1872, nearly 10 years before British India began to extend a settled administration there" (Pollock 1979:4).

Altogether, over 27 families served in Nagaland, spreading the gospel of Jesus Christ. Below are the missionaries who faithfully served in Nagaland.

1. Rev. and Mrs. Miles Bronson   1838–1841 Konyak Nagas

2. Edward Winter Clark, D.D.,
   and Mary Mead Clark   1872–1911 Ao

3. Rev. Charles De Witt King
   and Anna M. Sweet King   1878–1886 Angami

4. Sidney White Rivenburg, M.D.
   and Hattie Elizabeth Tiffany Rivenburg   1884–1908 Ao and Angami
   and second wife, Helen B. Protzman   1910–1916 Ao and Angami

5. William Ellsworth Witter, M.D., D.D.,   1885–1888 Lotha
   and Mary Potter Witter
   and second wife, Mary Barss Witter   1912–1923 Sibsagar,
                                              Gauhati & Jorhat Assam

6. Rev. Samuel Alden Perrine
   and Rose Ermina Perrine   1892–1905 Ao and Lotha

7. Fred Porter Haggard, D.D.,   1893–1899 Ao and Lotha
   and Fannie Lilian Snow Haggard

8. Willard Fox Dowd, M.D.,   1900–1920 Ao
   and Muriel Annette Massey Dowd

9. Walter. A Loops, M.D.
   and Vincey Preston Loops   1905–1909 Ao

10. Miss Ella Grey Miller   1902–1906 Ao

11. Rev. Robert Bell Longwell
    and Bernie Bellentine Longwell, R.N.   1906–1914 Ao and Lotha

12. Rev. Harry Byram Dickson
    and Eleanor Austin McAfee Dickson   1901–1908 Ao and Angami

13. Narola Elizabeth Rivenburg, Ph.D.   Ao and Angami

14. James Riley Bailey, M.D.
    and Anna Mary McClure Bailey   1910–1928 Ao and Lotha

15. William Carlson Smith, Ph.D.,
    and Enid Severy Smith   1912–1915 Ao

16. Rev. Joseph Eric Tanquist   1912–1940 Angami and
    and Mabel Christine Tanquist   Lotha

17. Miss Ethel May Stevenson   1918–1931 Ao

18. Miss Ethel Masales
    (Later married Rev. Pettegrew)   1919–1930 Ao

19. Miss Edna Mary Stever, R.N.	1920–1923 Ao
20. Rev. Geo Washington Supplee and Ruth Lamberton Supplee	1922–1949 Angami
21. Miss Augusta Maine Grisenhener	1915–1926 Ao
22. Rev. Roger.R. Wickstrand and Mrs. Wickstrand, R.N.	1929–1933 Ao
23. Rev. Bengt I. Anderson and Edna Anderson	1936–1948 Sema
24. Charles Earl Hunter, D.D. and Cleda Alldredge Hunter	1948–1950 Ao
25. Rev. A.S. Truxton and Ouida Fay Haskins Truxton	1952–1954 Ao
26. Rev. Robert Fletcher Delano	1949 Sema
27. Rev. Howard Houston and Harriet Jane Campbell Houston	1947–1954 Lotha and Angami

During the early days, many other missionaries also served at the Jorhat and Golaghat Mission School. One of them was Rev. Miriam Robinson, who taught at the Golaghat Girls School. Our family had the privilege of personally getting to know this incredible woman. On one of our visits, she gave me an Ao necklace, an Assamese brass container, and raw silk materials, which I treasure to this day. For many years we remained close friends until she went home to be with the Lord. Rev. Robinson visited us twice in California, and we often drove to see her in Fresno, where she resided at the San Joaquim Garden Home. In every conversation, she brought up her ministry in Golaghat and her visit to Nagaland. She reminisced about her ministry, where she had become acquainted with many of the Naga girls who came to study there. One of her students, Mrs. Mhalo Kikon from the Lotha Tribe, was able to meet with Rev. Robinson at our home in American Canyon. It was a privilege to get to know some of the missionaries who had been influential among the Nagas in the past.

Another dear friend who is an Ao Naga lady, Mrs. Pangila Walling of San Jose, California, told me that she had heard from her parents how Dr. Clark was the target of spears and daos by the Naga warriors but managed to escape unharmed. Truly, the throngs of angels protected the missionaries from the land of spears. Only someone called by the Lord and filled with the Holy Spirit would go to unknown territories to share the gospel of Jesus Christ.

The sacrifices of the missionaries are not forgotten, nor have they been wasted. Naga Christians are blessed, and we wonder in amazement at the love of God as we look back at how Christianity came to the Naga Hills. Every one of the missionaries who entered the Naga Hills risked their lives. Some succumbed to diseases, and one died at sea. They came to a poverty-stricken land and lived with the then head-hunting wild tribes who had no written languages.

Dr. Charles Earl Hunter, D.D., who served with his wife, Cleda Alldredge Hunter, as missionaries to the Ao Naga Tribe from 1948–1950, died at sea due to a heart attack, while returning on furlough with his wife, who was also ill, and their children, Paul Maxwell (four years old) and Beth Ellen (one and a half years old). Dr. Hunter died on December 24, 1950, aboard the S.S. City of Perth. He was buried at sea on Christmas Eve. How gut-wrenching such a tragedy must have been for Mrs. Hunter, who herself was not well, and for the children too. Living and serving in the Naga Hills as missionaries took a toll on their bodies and their mental health as well.

The British already inhabited the Naga Hills during this time and controlled the Nagas by fear and force. The American Baptist missionaries came and showed love and acceptance by educating the Nagas. Rev. Bengt Anderson reported that the deputy commissioner was courteous and friendly but not especially interested in the American missionaries (Anderson 1978:15).

The British were territorial, and the discovery of the Naga Tribes had been a significant anthropological find. Mr. J.P. Mills, a British officer and an author, wrote volumes of books documenting the culture, customary practices, and lifestyle of the Nagas in the eighteenth and the nineteenth century, which is a treasure for future generations of Nagas and the world. I give him praise for allowing the Nagas to get a glimpse of their past through his well-documented books.

Another British author, Mr. Verrier Elwin, who wrote the book *The Nagas in the Nineteenth Century*, was very appreciative of the American Baptist missionaries, calling them excellent and exemplary men who devoted their lives to the Nagas by bringing education, written languages, and awareness of the outside world. In his own words, Elwin eloquently described the Nagas and summed up the work of the missionaries as follows:

> A more general acquaintance with the people, and a more diligent attention to their languages, it is hoped, will not long be wanting to throw light on these interesting races. Already have two or three members of the American Baptist Board of Foreign missions established themselves in the Naga Hills, and has become so far acquainted with the language of the tribe amongst whom they have located themselves (the Namsangiyas), as to have been able to get up a few elementary books in that dialect, and to open a school for the education of the children. To the perseverance of these exemplary men, in the great cause to which they have devoted their lives, we shall soon be indebted for much and valuable information regarding the Naga tribes in general, and the products of the hills which they inhabit. It is further to be hoped, that by the blessing of the Divine Providence, through the efforts of these excellent men, the Nagas, who from time immemorial have seen the score and the prey of their more civilized neighbours may shortly begin to emerge from that dark barbarism which now renders the tribe of each hill an enemy to that of the next, and has hitherto prevented an Alpine tract of great natural resources and high fertility, from supporting more than a very scanty population of savages, in a state of discomfort and privation. (Elwin 1969–85).

As a result of the sacrifices, devotion and exemplary lives of the American Baptist missionaries who, residing practically in the jungle alongside the natives, invested their time, energy, and entire lives loving, teaching, nurturing, caring, and showing the love of Jesus to the then heathen Nagas, the Nagas today embrace the love of God and a love for education. In most Naga households, college education is not optional, so Nagaland now has many highly educated young people. English is the medium of instruction and the official language in Nagaland.

The gospel according to John 3:16 (NIV):

For God so loved the world that he gave his one and only Son, that whoever believes in him shall not perish but have eternal life.

God so loved the Nagas that He sent the American Baptist missionaries to liberate the Nagas by sharing the good news of the gift of eternal life through Jesus Christ and release from the terrible bondage and fearful living of headhunting. How amazing is God's grace and mercy!

◇◇◇◇◇◇◇◇◇◇

Chapter 22[1]
Prædicans ad Confluentes[2]

I N 1905, TRENTON JUNCTION had a most exotic visitor, from far
away Nagaland, a province found in the jewel of the British Empire's
crown, India. Located in the northeastern corner of that country,
Nagaland borders Burma and it is one of modern India's smallest
states. Surrounded by Hinduism and Buddhism, Nagaland is mostly
(88 percent) Christian.

Around 1887, a boy named Eramo Shanjamo Jungi was born in
Nagaland. He was of the Lota tribe and, in 1905, he became the first
Naga to come to the United States and receive a foreign education.

Mrs. S.A. Parrine was the wife of a Baptist minister and the daugh-
ter of Rev. and Mrs. M.T. Lamb of Grand Avenue, in Trenton Junction.
She and her husband were Baptist missionaries sent to Nagaland. On
December 27, 1904, they brought Shanjamo back to the United States.
He spent 1905 living with the Lambs in their farmhouse on Grand
Avenue, and he spent the school year studying at the Trenton Junction
public school, just down the road.

On October 27, 1905, the Rev. Judson Conklin, of the Clinton
Avenue Baptist Church in Trenton, arranged to have Shanjamo lecture
about his home. Mrs. Parrine interpreted for him.

---

1. (chapter 22 & 23 from the book *One Square Mile* used with permission from the author
Mark W. Falzini) Falzini, Mark W. *One Square Mile. A History of Trenton Junction, New
Jersey*. iUniverse, Bloomington, IN. 2017
2. Latin for: *Preaching at the Junction*

The following year, Shanjamo transferred to a school in Port Norris and finally, in 1907, he transferred to the Mt. Hermon School in Warren County. He returned to Nagaland on November 27, 1908. He was very active in the Baptist Church in India, was ordained, established churches and preached at many churches throughout his homeland. He died in 1956.

Today in Nagaland, there is a monument to Eramo Shanjamo Jungi, highlighting the fact that he was the first of his people to receive a foreign education. On the monument is a plaque with his photograph and a list of all of his accomplishments in life and as a Baptist minister and missionary. Included in this vast list is his stay in Trenton Junction.[3]

Religion was a very important component of life in Trenton Junction at the turn of the century. The first European settlers in the area were Baptists, Presbyterians and Episcopalians. The Roman Catholic population was very tiny until the advent of the railroads—and the arrival of immigrant railroad workers from Italy.

Initially, there was no actual church building in Trenton Junction for any religion. Episcopalians met in private homes, usually after seven o'clock on Sunday evenings. They never developed more than a mission in Trenton Junction, which was known as *St. Alban's Mission.* The closest Episcopal Church was built on Prospect Street in Ewing Township after the turn of the century.

The origin of the Presbyterian Church in Trenton Junction stretches back to 1845 when the church was initially organized as the *Birmingham Sunday School.* At that time, classes were held "in the old stone school house" and were directed by the Rev. Eli Field Cooley of Ewing Presbyterian Church.

When the railroad arrived in 1876, and Birmingham was renamed Trenton Junction, the Sunday School was also renamed the *Trenton Junction Sunday School.* It was not until 1906 when the school was incorporated as the Trenton Junction Community Church. At that

---

3. Falzini, Mark. *West Trenton's Connection to* India. *Archival Ramblings.* September 2016. http://njspmuseum.blogspot.com/2016/09/west-trentons-connection-to-india.html.

time, "Grange Hall on Grand Avenue was purchased and used for Sunday School and Church purposes."

In 1918, property on the corner of Grand and Trenton Avenues was donated by Trenton attorney, Isaac Richey, for use as a church site. The following year, "the congregation bought additional adjoining property." It would still be more than a decade before an actual church building would be erected.

When the new Trenton Junction train station changed its name to West Trenton, so too did the West Trenton Presbyterian Church. In April 1931, a Loyalty Campaign was begun to help raise the $25,000 needed for the construction of a permanent stone church. Throughout the month of April, special prayer services, meetings and lectures, and dinners were held to raise additional funds.

Construction finally began in May. The church was "a brownstone structure of Norman Gothic architecture, with a belfry, bell, and cathedral windows. The bell was presented to the church by the Ladies' Aid Society in 1932." The new church had enough seating for 150 congregants. A church hall was also built, with Sunday School rooms located in the basement. Services began being held in the church in October 1932.[4]

When the Italian immigrants moved into Trenton Junction to work on the railroad, there were no Roman Catholic churches nearby. They would take the trolley into Trenton to attend Mass at St. Joachim's Church—Trenton's Italian parish.

In 1915, Joseph Croce asked the diocese to send a priest to Trenton Junction. The Bishop of Trenton agreed, and he assigned a priest to celebrate Mass each Sunday at six o'clock in the morning on Croce's porch. Unfortunately, during inclement weather, Mass was cancelled.[5] Nuns were dispatched from St. Joachim's to instruct the children in Catechism and prepare them for Confirmation.

---

4. "Inventory of the Church Archives of New Jersey: Presbyterians." Newark, NJ: The Historical Records Survey, 1940; Trenton Evening Times, April 3, 1931.
5. Tesauro, JoAnn. "Images of America: Ewing Township, New Jersey." Arcadia Publishers, 2002, page 40.

An empty building owned by Frank Roma of Philadelphia that was located in the center of the railroad camp was secured and converted into a makeshift church. "It was a tin garage and was heated by a potbellied stove. In the summer, the doors were left open and goats and chickens would wander in during Mass." The first Mass was celebrated in the new church on Palm Sunday, April 24, 1918.

Eventually, the congregation outgrew the makeshift church. Sometime in the 1930s, a new parish church, Our Lady of Good Counsel, was built on Grand Avenue, just north of Summit Avenue, where the Post Office is currently located. In 1963, the parish moved again. The new church was built on what was once George Hunt's farm at the edge of Trenton Junction's original boundary, where West Upper Ferry Road and Wilburtha Road merge. Because the old church building could not be sold or repurposed, it was decided to burn the building and allow the fire department to use the event as a drill. [6]

---

6. Michael J. Falzini. *Interview with the author.* May 12, 1991 and John "Jake" Garzio. *Interview with the author.* May 12, 1991.

Chapter 23 [1]
Sing Praises

T HE FOLLOWING IS a letter sent to the editor of the *Trenton Evening Times* by "J.M.A." of Trenton Junction. It was published one hundred and ten years ago, on November 12, 1906. It speaks to high quality of life in Trenton Junction both then, and now:

To the Editor of the Times:

Sir—It has been noticed recently that many towns have been boasting through the press of their many superior qualities and inducements. After observing and absorbing the good features which has been set forth, the writer of this article feels that Trenton Junction is not by any means in the background, but is rather on the alert and abreast with the march of progress in various ways.

As a residence section it is far superior to any town within a radius of fifty or more miles from Trenton, owing to its location, altitude, natural drainage, pure air and pure water, all of these being the essentials of a home. The place is just far enough away to avoid factory smoke and the general noise of a great city, and for the man with daily business in New York,

---

1. (chapter 22 & 23 from the book *One Square Mile* used with permission from the author Mark W. Falzini) Falzini, Mark W. *One Square Mile. A History of Trenton Junction, New Jersey*. iUniverse, Bloomington, IN. 2017

Philadelphia or Trenton, it is only a matter of a short ride via the steam railroad or trolley.

The grocer, baker, milkman and butcher are in daily attendance to supply the desires of the inner man. Telephones, with the advantage of unlimited service in the Trenton circuit, are to be had at a moderate cost per year.

Public school facilities equal to city schools with promotion of pupils to the Trenton High School, at the cost of the local district, are also available.

The tax rate this year is only $1.01.

An improvement society has been organized by the broad minded men of the community for the purpose of improving conditions generally, and already many important matters have been considered and disposed of successfully, much to its credit.

A physician, with one of the most complete offices in this State, containing the most modern X-Ray and electrical equipment and generating his own power, is here.

Patients from New York, Pennsylvania and many sections of New Jersey seek treatment at this place and many cures have been recorded. Cancers have been removed entirely under this electrical treatment, while the patient suffers little or no pain. Many students have sought knowledge here.

All these conditions go far toward making an ideal home for a busy man and his family.

J.M.A.

Trenton Junction, Nov. 10, 1906

◇◇◇◇◇◇◇◇◇◇

West Trenton

*formerly known as Birmingham
and Trenton Junction, New Jersey*

S HANJAMO FIRST ARRIVED at Trenton Junction with the Perrine's and attended Trenton Junction public school in New Jersey. In the first edition of this book, Trenton Junction now known as West Trenton was not documented as I could not find detailed information until I read the book *One Square Mile* by Mark W. Falzini of West Trenton. In his book Falzini documented the visit of Shanjamo Jungi to Trenton Junction now called West Trenton.

Mark W. Falzini, a historian, archivist, author and a resident of Trenton Junction now called West Trenton documented that "In 1905, Trenton Junction had a most exotic visitor, from far away Nagaland, a province found in the jewel of the British Empire's crown, India. Located in the northeastern corner of that country." (Falzini 2017:143). He further stated that Mrs. Rose Ermina Perrine was the daughter of a Baptist minister the Rev. and Mrs. M.T Lamb of Grand Avenue, in Trenton Junction. Falzini documented Shanjamo arriving in the United States in December 1904 and spent the year 1905 living with the Lambs in their farmhouse on Grand Avenue and attended Trenton Junction public school. Falzini gave an account that on October 27, 1905, Shanjamo was invited to speak at the Clinton Avenue Baptist Church in Trenton Junction by the Rev. Judson Conklin about his homeland which Mrs. Perrine interpreted for him. This is a rare treasure to get a glimpse of Shanjamo's early days living in Trenton

Junction now known as West Trenton, New Jersey in the United States. Trenton Junction changed its name to West Trenton on June 1st 1931.

Trenton Junction public school is about 2 blocks from the farmhouse Shanjamo resided on Grand Avenue with the Lambs. According to Falzini, the original school was a one storied building. Apparently the school burnt down in 1916 damaging the interior but fortunately the structure was not destroyed. In 1916, Mark W. Falzini's paternal grandparents Vincenzo (Jimmy) and Ubaldina (Pauline) Falzini bought the school and added the upper story making it a two story home. The family lived there from 1916–1983. The Falzinis immigrated from Italy. The building is now home to "Princeton Mortgage." After attending Trenton Junction public school, Shanjamo attended Port Norris public school where Rev. Samuel Alden Perrine accepted a call to be the pastor at Port Norris Baptist church, New Jersey.

As a guest of Mark W. Falzini, it was a real treat to visit the farmhouse Shanjamo lived with the Lambs 115 years ago when he first arrived at Trenton Junction. The farmhouse still stands in its original structure and beauty. The Lambs sold the house to the McConahay's who still resides till today.

Clinton Avenue Baptist church where Shanjamo was invited to speak by the Rev. Judson Conklin still stands. According to Falzini, it was the Rev. Judson Conklin who married his maternal grandparents in 1927. Mark W. Falzini's family worshipped at the Clinton Avenue Baptist church in the late 1920s–1970s. The congregation had a membership close to 1,000. It was a thriving ministry under Rev. Judson Conklin. For Shanjamo to have spoken about his homeland in front of thousands is remarkable. The congregation must have been intrigued to learn about the people in the Naga Hills from him. He could have spoken in English, Lotha, Ao, Sema or Assamese languages that he was fluent in. Mrs. Perrine, who interpreted for him, having lived and worked in the Naga Hills and responsible for translating the Bible into the Naga languages along with her husband was also fluent in these languages. Indeed, it is remarkable to learn of the confidence Shanjamo Jungi had in preaching in front of such a large audience. Preaching was truly his passion.

Clinton Ave Baptist church closed its doors on December 28, 1969 due to a decline in membership leading to a financial crisis. Under a new name called the Jerusalem Baptist Church opened its doors the following April in 1970. Jerusalem Baptist still stands today. The original steeple fell during a heavy wind in the 1900s.

The farmhouse residence of Rev. & Mrs. M.T Lamb (parents of Mrs. Rose Ermina Lamb Perrine). Shanjamo lived here with the Perrine's in Trenton Junction now known as West Trenton, New Jersey. The Lambs sold the house to the McConahay's who are the current residents of this beautiful home.

Trenton Junction public school where Shanjamo attended when he first arrived in the United States. Originally, it was only a one story building.

The original church of Clinton Baptist Avenue church where the Reverend Judson Conklin invited Shanjamo to lecture about his homeland.

Clinton Avenue Baptist Church is now known as the Jerusalem Baptist Church. West Trenton, New Jersey

Rev. Samuel Alden Perrine, B.S., B.Th., and Rose Ermina Lamb Perrine

Port Norris, New Jersey

T HE PERRINES WERE responsible for bringing Shanjamo to study in the United States. Rev. S.A. Perrine was born in Greensburg, Indiana, on February 19, 1859. He was baptized in Centralia, Illinois, in 1875. He subsequently became a member of the First Baptist Church in Marshalltown, Iowa, and later attended Shurtleff College, Chicago University, and the Chicago University Divinity School. He married Rose Ermina Lamb on June 9, 1891. They had two children, Linden LaRue and Caroline Lucile.

The Perrines were assigned to serve in the Naga Hills by the American Baptist Mission on March 28, 1892. With the help of Shanjamo and Chichamo, the Perrines translated many texts into the Lotha Naga language, including the Gospel of Matthew, the Lord's Prayer, the child's prayer, and many hymns.

The Perrines were especially interested in educating the Naga youths, and as there were no written languages, they worked hard to produce texts for all the tribes. Mrs. Perrine's health declined during their mission work in Nagaland. As a result, they returned to the States. Accompanying them was young Shanjamo. Mr. Perrine accepted the call as pastor at Port Norris Baptist Church in New Jersey and served from July 14, 1906, through May 9, 1909. In 1909, Rev. Perrine served as the pastor of the Fifth Baptist Church of Newark, in New Jersey.

Port Norris during the late 1800s and early 1900s was a thriving town due to the profitable oyster industry. Many different members of Port Norris Baptist Church told me that during the heyday of the oyster industry, there were more millionaires in Port Norris than in any other city in the state. The oyster industry provided many jobs and much revenue. As we drove around town, we saw beautiful, majestic homes in Port Norris, a reminder of the affluent days of long ago.

Shanjamo attended Port Norris Public School, and according to records. The building that once housed the school at Port Norris is still standing and is now Port Norris Robbinstown Public Library. It was easy to visualize a young Shanjamo living, working, studying, and preaching in Port Norris. I was overwhelmed with nostalgia as I thought that over 100 years earlier, this had been Shanjamo's school, and I was now privileged to experience it firsthand. Today the library is used for adult education, poetry readings, and other community activities.

Shanjamo routinely acknowledged that God had brought him to the United States so that he could receive a better education. His faith in God gave him tremendous courage and strength to continue his studies, despite his distance from home.

Port Norris was not a diverse society in those days, so as a foreigner, Shanjamo stood out because of the color of his skin. In his letters, he acknowledged the struggles and discrimination he experienced, but his deep faith in the Lord sustained him. He quoted the Scriptures in many of his letters, and in the verses he found both strength and resilience. Shanjamo had a clear understanding of Jesus, and this inspired him to remain dedicated and devoted to his studies in spite of adversities. As you read his letters, you will recognize his understanding and grasp of English language. One cannot help but admire him for his courage and his love for the Lord. He was a sincere follower of Jesus Christ.

Western cuisine must have been a challenge for Shanjamo in the beginning. Even after living in the United States for many years, I still long for the local pork of Nagaland, cooked in bamboo shoots with hot chilies and local spices (a well-known Naga dish). Thankfully, I can get all of the ingredients in the Chinese and the Korean markets today. In the early 1900s, America was not as diverse; therefore, there weren't many choices for ethnic food, meaning Shanjamo would have had to adjust quickly to American cuisine and lifestyle.

The First Baptist Church in Port Norris, where the Perrines pastored and Shanjamo worshipped, still stands and currently has about 100 church members. I had the opportunity to worship there on Easter Sunday in April 2017, another unforgettable event of my life. As I sat and worshipped our risen Lord on that beautiful Easter morning, my heart raced once again with mixed emotions. I was teary-eyed as I quietly said a prayer of thanksgiving to God for allowing me to be in the church where Shanjamo had worshipped. Again, I could imagine Shanjamo as a young man sitting in the pew, singing and listening to Rev. Perrine give his sermons. Our hosts, Ken and LaDawn Wilford, were very accommodating and made it possible for my husband and me to visit Port Norris and worship along with them. Ken serves as a Sunday school teacher, and he is also the associate pastor. His wife LaDawn is the pianist of the church. Ken's parents, Ken Wilford, Sr., and his wife Jeanne invited us into their home for Easter lunch. It was a treat and a blessing for us to enjoy a delicious, home-cooked meal during this holy time. The Wilfords live in Millville, New Jersey, a small town Shanjamo frequented, about a 20-minute drive from Port Norris.

Rev. Samuel Alden Perrine and Rose Ermina Lamb Perrine served in the Naga Hills amongst the Ao Naga Tribe and the Lotha Naga Tribe 1892–1905

Dr. Edwin Winter Clark & Mrs. Mary Mead Clark (Missionary to the Ao Nagas from 1872-1911), responsible for sending Shanjamo Jungi to the United States with Rev. Samuel Alden Perrine and Mrs. Rose Ermina Lamb Perrine

The original Port Norris Public School, New Jersey, where Shanjamo attended. (Courtesy Port Norris Public Library)

A current picture of the Port Norris Public School building, now the Port Norris Robbinstown Public Library

Picture of Port Norris Baptist Church New Jersey
where Shanjamo worshipped

Interior, Port Norris Baptist Church, New Jersey

◇◇◇◇◇◇◇◇◇◇◇

Northfield Mount Hermon School

F ROM PORT NORRIS, we headed to Mt. Hermon School in North-field, Massachusetts, and stayed in the beautiful town of Green-field. This town is where Shanjamo went to see Dr. Benjamin Croft for his eye appointments. Out of curiosity, we drove down Federal Street to see if any of the descendants of Dr. Croft still practice op-tometry. Today Federal Street ends in the 600 block, and we found no signs of any optometry offices.

We visited Mt. Hermon School in Northfield, where Shanjamo attended for two years, and were greeted warmly by Mr. Peter Weis, the soft-spoken archivist of the school. Mr. Weis generously shared all of the documents from Shanjamo's files, which were beautifully and carefully preserved. Our meeting was a joyous one after a few years of correspondence through emails and phone calls.

Mt. Hermon is a prestigious school, co-ed since the fall of 1971. In 1906, there were 667 students, with 144 international attendees; among those, four were from India. The tuition fee at the time was $50 per term, and additional fees of $5 per service were charged to cover laundry, nurse visits, and physical education. The students also con-tributed $5 to cover the purchase of books, writing materials, clothes, and travel expenses. Work study was available for students to earn and support their expenses.

Shanjamo must have felt at home in Northfield since the terrain is mountainous and the weather mild and pleasant, similar to that of Nagaland. The winter snow must have been quite a delight for him to experience, as Nagaland does not have a snowy season.

Adjusting to different cultural norms was likely difficult for Shanjamo. Naga society is a very close-knit community, and villagers rely on each other for day-to-day roles and activities. In this culture, hospitality and generosity are practiced and valued; guests show up at any time and often stay for long periods. Conversely, America is an individualistic society, where a tremendous respect for privacy is the way of life. In American culture, people do not show up at the door without making an appointment, and guests rarely overstay their welcome.

Shanjamo was sponsored by Mrs. Irene Gardner Ropes of Morristown, New Jersey, an affluent community in the area. She graciously offered to pay Shanjamo's expenses and tuition fees. We went to Morristown, New Jersey, hoping to locate the home of Mrs. Ropes, although the home no longer exists.

The Mount Hermon campus is pristine and breathtaking, and we strolled around, enjoying its beauty and the natural surroundings. I once again reflected on what it must have been like for Shanjamo as he walked these same steps 100 years ago. I commend the bravery and adventurous spirit of this brilliant man and follower of the Lord who came all this way to study in order to offer a new path for those in his native land.

The Mount Hermon Boys School was founded by D.L. Moody with the mission to train young men for the ministry. The curriculum was intense and well-rounded, with numerous subjects in the curriculum: Bible study, Greek and Latin, English, math, algebra, geometry, trigonometry, French, physiology, zoology, botany, physics, landscaping, gardening and forestry, agriculture, horticulture, animal husbandry, history, science, and literature. There was also an industrial department, where each student was required to work thirteen and one half hours each week. Here students were taught carpentry, plumbing, blacksmithing, and painting. Also on the school's premises was a farm that housed livestock—including cows, horses, sheep, pigs, and chickens. A vegetable and fruit garden provided a hands-on experience in the fields of agriculture and horticulture.

According to Nicole Hager, the dean of students of Mount Hermon School: "Many schools profess to educate the whole child. At NMH [Northfield Mount Herman], we live and breathe our founder's motto to educate the heads, hearts, and hands of young people. I came to NMH—as perhaps you will, too—because part of the school's mission is to encourage students to live with purpose and to make a difference in the world." The mission of Northfield Mount Hermon is: "Dig deep, work hard, be real, what it means to be well-grounded."

Northfield farm 1912 (Courtesy Northfield Mount Hermon Archives)

Northfield Mount Hermon School entrance welcome sign

The dorm where Shanjamo resided

Crossley Hall Dormitory (modern). According to Mr. Peter Weis, the archivist of Northfield Mount Hermon, Shanjamo may have resided here as well.

The chapel of Northfield Mount Hermon

Northfield Mount Hermon admissions office (modern)

Northfield Mount Hermon Blake Hall (modern)

Northfield Mount Hermon campus as it is today
(Courtesy Northfield Mount Hermon)

Dr. Henry Franklin Cutler

1862–1945

D
R. CUTLER WAS the third principal of Mt. Hermon School, and he took great interest in Shanjamo while he was a student there. Even after Shanjamo's departure to Nagaland, the two corresponded. Dr. Cutler was a kind, encouraging, and practical professor and principal. He had a tremendous influence on Shanjamo throughout his life. Shanjamo regarded Dr. Cutler as his mentor. After his return to Nagaland, Shanjamo proved to be a disciplined, hardworking, and diligent preacher who tirelessly and faithfully shared the Word of God with his people.

Mt. Hermon School was a competitive environment, offering a challenging curriculum. Even today it is difficult to be granted admission. The admission application states: "Feeble minds with no aptitude for study and feeble bodies with no power of endurance are excluded, not because they need no help, but because the school is not adapted to this class of pupils. Lazy boys are not desired."

I have included a portion of Mr. Cutler's story in this book to emphasize his influence and importance in Shanjamo's life. It is also my desire that young Nagas will be inspired by Mr. Cutler's hard work and devotion and go on to lead lives of meaningful and lasting value.

The most important stage of a person's life is early childhood. The way we are raised influences how we think and behave in later years. Mr. Cutler's biography reveals the strong work ethic and values emphasized by his loving Christian parents. His life story shows how essential it is that we teach good work ethics so that our children will grow up to be contributing citizens in society. In our Naga culture, the boys are not expected to help with household chores, whereas the girls are tasked with chores, such as cleaning, cooking, fetching water, collecting firewood, and babysitting. Naga culture defines cooking and household chores as the duties of women, while the few men who do help with household duties are frowned upon and ridiculed. In most cases, men only enter the kitchen when it is time to eat or during tea time.

The Naga people still need to learn the importance of discontinuing these practices. Both boys and girls should be treated equally, teaching them good work habits to pass on to future generations.

Mary Mead Clark documented that as she and her husband travelled to the Naga Hills, people were assigned to carry their belongings. The chief men were there, but they did not lend a helping hand. Mrs. Clark stated: "Oh, no! This would be much beneath their dignity" (M.M. Clark 1907:29). Nothing should be beneath us if we want to get the job done, achieve our goal, and be successful in life. Because Naga pride still exists, the young generation must be careful to practice a "can do" attitude to achieve a successful future.

Henry Franklin Cutler was born on May 27, 1862. His parents, Daniel Smith Cutler and Adaline Sibley Cutler, lived in Greenwich, Massachusetts. Henry Cutler believed in educating youth; he was a godly man, as well as a hard-working citizen. His attitude and outlook were made possible by the contributions of his parents, who taught him the joy and benefits of hard work. According to his biographer, Richard Ward Day:

> Henry was taught early that he must never be wasteful of time. From dawn until sundown there were jobs to do. His jobs included sawing and chopping wood, milking the twelve cows, feeding the pigs, and caring for the calves, the two horses, the steers, and seventy-five hens. There were moreover, two large vegetable gardens to be cared for. Each season made its own demands: the hay to be scythed, piled in rows, and brought

into the barn: or the oats, buckwheat, and field corn to be cut: or the walnut trees in the field behind the barn, and the chestnut tree in the Prescott field, to be poled (Day 1950:13).

His days as a young boy foreshadow the dedicated, hardworking, and well-disciplined man he grew into. In addition, his upbringing shows the conscientiousness of his parents, who taught him obedience and courtesy. Because of the training he received as a youth growing up on a farm, he developed confidence and courage in the workforce, as well as in his personal life.

At a very early age, Henry was taught by his father the value of money and of making every penny count. Henry was a wonderful man, calm in nature and rarely losing his temper. As a result, he was socially engaging and had many friends throughout his life. Henry also had a thirst for knowledge and learned to play the violin. His teacher, Miss Jessie E. Smith, encouraged him and inspired him to seek further education. On August 21, 1877, Henry Cutler arrived at New Salem Academy. His older sister Mary joined him at New Salem, where they were self-boarders for the first year, which means they had to gather firewood and food, as well as cook all by themselves. It is reported that Henry even baked his own bread.

While at New Salem, Henry met another amazing teacher by the name of William H. Smiley, a graduate of Harvard University. Mr. Smiley instilled in Henry a love of learning. In Henry's own words: "Principal Smiley gave me a love for Latin and an increased desire to go to College. More important still, he gave me great help in those days, when I needed encouragement and directions" (Day 1950:26).

During Henry's college years, he worked to support himself. Even during school holidays, he would work, earning extra money to pay for his tuition. He graduated from Amherst College on June 30, 1886.

Henry joined the teaching staff at Mt. Hermon School in the fall of 1886. He took a leave to study in Europe for two years and became a language scholar of Latin, French, German, Greek, Italian, and Spanish. In the fall of 1889, he taught at the West Chester Academy in Pennsylvania. While at Mt. Hermon School he had met Harriet Louise Ford, and the two were married on July 23, 1890. Shortly after, D.L. Moody, the founder of Mt. Hermon School, asked Cutler to become the principal. Dr. Moody's vision was that young men trained at Mt. Hermon School would be evangelists, teaching the good news of Jesus Christ all over the world and becoming strong Christian influences in their communities. Mr. Cutler believed in Dr. Moody's vision and accepted the invitation to become the principal of Mt. Hermon.

Dr. Moody encouraged the expulsion of students who were not benefiting from the school. Only those who showed progress and appreciated the privilege of growing and learning at Mount Hermon were given the opportunity to continue their studies. Because Mr. Cutler was extremely efficient in executing his duties as the principal, the school gained popularity and recognition.

D.L. Moody died on December 26, 1899. At Mt. Hermon, Dr. Cutler continued the original mission of Dr. Moody and encouraged the students to lead better lives with a higher standard of conduct. During chapel time, he often told students that: "A tree is known by its fruit," and "A good tree bringeth forth good fruit." Cutler often quoted Luke 12:48, KJV: *"For unto whomsoever much is given, of him shall be much required"* (Day 1950:120).

He continued to preach the love and forgiveness of Jesus, emphasizing how a life can change through understanding and acceptance. Through God everything is made possible if we put our trust in Him. Under Dr. Cutler's leadership, Mount Hermon students received not only an excellent education, but also an understanding of living a Christian life and evangelizing communities.

Shanjamo was deeply influenced by the teachings of Dr. Cutler, who had heard of the Naga Hills from Dr. Witter and the Perrines. Because of this, he made sure Shanjamo was fully prepared and equipped before his return home. Mrs. Perrine mentioned in one of her letters that Dr. Cutler invited Shanjamo to his house for dinner along with Dr. Witter. It must have been a joyful evening at the Cutlers' residence, where Shanjamo was reunited with Dr. Witter, who was on a sabbatical and study leave.

Shanjamo had been a student at the Impur School, where Dr. Clark ran the school and the ministry. It must have been a glorious and joyous evening for both Dr. Witter and Shanjamo to reminisce about their time together in Nagaland. Dr. Witter and his wife Mary had spent time at Impur as well, before they were assigned to the Lotha Tribe of the Wokha Hills.

Dr. Witter spent many years in Nagaland as the first missionary to the Lotha Naga Tribe. He and his wife Mary Amelia Potter Witter served among the Lotha Tribe, and their son Volney Theodore Witter was born in Kohima, Nagaland. In 1888 the Witter family resided in Chicago so that Dr. Witter could study medicine. Dr. Witter obtained his Doctor of Medicine from the Chicago Homeopathic Hospital in 1890. He also received a similar degree from Hannaman Medical College in later years. The goal of the Witters was to finish school and return to the Naga Hills to continue their ministry; however, Mary Potter Witter suffered continued ill health, which postponed their plan indefinitely. She died due to an illness on April 1, 1911.

Later Dr. Witter married his second wife, Mary Barss Witter, who accompanied him to the Naga Hills during his second term. Dr. Witter and his first wife Mary Amelia Potter's son Volney Theodore Witter served as a missionary in South India. I had the privilege of meeting the two daughters of Volney Theodore: Vera Witter Hodge and Barbara Witter. We have remained close friends with Bill and Ted Hodge, sons of Vera Witter Hodge.

Dr. Cutler and his wife, Harriet Ford Cutler, had seven children, four boys and three girls. Harriet was outgoing, cheerful, social, and influential. They both believed in manual labor, so the children were each given chores to fulfill. They grew their own fruits and vegetables and canned them. Breakfast was served at seven in the morning followed by a blessing and devotion. During devotion, Dr. Cutler would read passages from the Bible, and verses were memorized.

Each child played at least one instrument, and the family would gather to play music together, with Dr. Cutler joining them on his violin. He always encouraged his children to live a productive life and never waste time. He greatly depended on Harriet for support, and together they were instrumental in making Mount Hermon thrive. Unfortunately, Harriet had a weak heart, and she died young, leaving Dr. Cutler a widower with their seven children.

Shortly after Harriet's death, Dr. Cutler was conferred the Doctor of Civil Laws from the University of Syracuse, New York. He married Carrie Bell Cutler in 1907. She took care of the children and became a beloved member of the family until January 14, 1926, when she died suddenly and unexpectedly. Dr. Cutler later married Mabel Learoyd in East Orange, New Jersey. Mabel had been a student of Harriet Ford Cutler, Dr. Cutler's first wife. Mabel taught mathematics at Mt. Hermon until her marriage to Dr. Cutler.

After he retired at the age of 70 as the principal of Mount Hermon, Dr. Cutler decided to pursue medicine at the University of Paris. At 78 years of age, he was the oldest medical student to graduate from the University of Vienna. In the spring of 1945, Dr. Cutler had a painful fall that confined him to his bed. He died October 8, 1945, with his wife by his side at Brattleboro Hospital. He was a great man, always willing to help, encourage, and bless others. It is no wonder Shanjamo revered him and looked to him for guidance, support, and encouragement.

From historical documents, we can clearly see that Dr. Cutler and Rev. Perrine were fully invested in Shanjamo. Proper training and education at Mt. Hermon gave Shanjamo the ability to return home to educate and evangelize the people of the Naga Hills. Upon returning to his homeland, Shanjamo didn't waste time in sharing the gospel of Jesus Christ. He knew that he had been chosen by God to study in the United States. Through my research, I determined that he was an enthusiastic servant of the Lord, preaching the Word of God tirelessly.

An immeasurable amount of love was shown to Shanjamo by Dr. Cutler, the Perrines, Sarah and Irene Ropes (Shanjamo's sponsors), Dr. Croft (Shanjamo's optometrist), and many others who helped him succeed. We all should embrace and practice the living of a meaningful and joyful life, lifting up one another and helping one another succeed. Jesus said to love one another; as followers of Jesus, we can see the power of love, as Christ taught us, demonstrated in the lives of these faithful people. In the midst of the many injustices in this world, we see love without borders or barriers, a great lesson to emulate.

Dr. Henry Franklin Cutler, Principal of Northfield
Mount Hermon mentor and friend of Shanjamo
(Courtesy of Northfield Mount Hermon Archives)

Shanjamo's Ministry in the Naga Hills

◇◇◇◇◇◇◇◇◇◇

S HANJAMO LEFT THE United States on September 10, 1908, and arrived at Gauhati, Assam on November 21. He reached Impur, Naga Hills, on November 27, 1908 (Kinghen 1972:15).

After his return to Nagaland, he preached the gospel of Jesus Christ to the local tribes. To be fluent in several languages is admirable; however, to be able to preach in different languages is even more appreciated. It shows that he was a gifted preacher, an evangelist, a teacher, and a gifted linguist as well. Mr. N.L. Kinghen (Kinghen 1972:14), documented that Shanjamo was fluent in the Ao language, both in preaching and singing. He also spoke the Assamese language fluently.

Upon his return from the United States to the Naga Hills, Shanjamo was actively involved in the ministry. Shanjamo was called back to Impur in 1909 to assist the American Baptist missionaries and also taught at the Impur Mission Center.

In subsequent years, he offered his services as pastor in several villages, including Changtongya Baptist Church (Ao Tribe), Yikhum Baptist Church (Lotha Tribe), Old Changsu Baptist Church (Lotha Tribe), and Littami Baptist Church (Sema Tribe). He also became a teacher at the Vankhosung Mission Center, where he taught from 1930 through 1937. He, along with Dr. Bailey, was one of the initial leaders of the school and donated Rupees 100 for the purchase and establishment of the center. He went back to his home village at Yikhum for a few years, and later he was called back to continue teaching at the Vankhosung Mission Center until 1948.

Shanjamo served as the pastor of Changtongya Baptist Church (Ao Tribe) from 1909–1910.

According to the Houstons, in 1910, Shanjamo became the interim associate to the pastor of Okotso Baptist Church (Lotha Tribe).

Shanjamo served as the pastor at Changbang Village Baptist Church (Lotha Tribe) from 1912 through 1913.

He served as the pastor at Yikhum Village Baptist Church in 1914, where he preached for one year.

From 1915–1917, he returned to Impur Mission Center (Ao Tribe) to lead the choirs and assist the American Baptist missionaries.

In March 1917, Shanjamo led the Naga Labour Corps to France during World War I.

In 1918, after his return one year later, he arrived in Kohima and worked closely with the deputy commissioner of the British Colonial government as a translator and accounts clerk, submitting accounts and records and disbursing payments to war veterans.

From 1919–1920, he served again as the pastor of Yikhum Village Baptist Church (Lotha Tribe). Shanjamo was from Yikhum village where he served as the pastor of the church two times. He eventually returned to his village where he spent his retirement years. He was laid to rest at Yikhum village. A beautiful church is constructed at Yikhum village and the Village people gather in the newly constructed church to worship Christ the Lord.

He served as the pastor of Old Changsu Baptist Church (Lotha Tribe) from 1921–1922. Old Changsu village is not far from Yikhum village. A beautiful church now stands overlooking the beautiful village, a testament of the work of the Holy Spirit and the faithful labor of the early Christians.

After his ministry at Changsu Village, he went to Littami Village (Sema Tribe), where he served as their first pastor from 1927–1929. During my visit to Nagaland in the summer of 2019, I visited the beautiful village of Old Littami to see where Shanjamo once served. We were greeted by Rev. Kitovi Assumi, the senior pastor, and Pastor

Atoka Sumi, the children's minister. Pastor Kitovi showed us their beautiful church. The current population of the village is around 400 residents. We spent close to an hour sharing information at the church guest house, where a picture of Shanjamo hung on the wall. A list of the names of the pastors who have served at Littami Baptist church was also displayed. It was heartwarming to see Shanjamo's name listed as their first pastor. As I stood outside the church and embraced the beauty of the village, I could not help but visualize Shanjamo, along with Rev. Bengt Anderson and his family, who had lived and served at Littami Village over 100 years ago. As a result of their work for Christ, a beautiful church now stands in which the people can worship the mighty God.

After pastoring in several villages, Pastor Shanjamo taught at the Vankhosung Mission School from 1930–1937. According to Yikhum Jubilee, Shanjamo was designated to be in charge of the Vankhosung Mission Center as a caretaker of the campus from 1948 through 1952. During this time, he was given a salary of five rupees per month. He ultimately retired in Yikhum Village, and at the age of 74 on Tuesday, February 28, 1956, he went home to be with the Lord.

Shanjamo was sought out as a pastor during this time and traveled frequently preaching the Word of Jesus Christ. He visited Mekukla, Tssori, L. Longidang and Lakhuti villages in the Lotha area amongst others, tirelessly and joyfully connecting with villagers and imparting to them the love and wisdom found through Christianity. In those days, no transportation was available. The only means of transportation was walking from one village to the next on foot. Travelers carried their rations in bamboo baskets on their backs.

In a letter to Dr. Cutler after returning from the United States, Shanjamo wrote from Changsu Village on August 28, 1922, that he had to march to Wokha in search of foreign stamps, which took him three hours each way. From Changsu Village to Wokha is an hour drive today. He described in his letter that there was no post office readily available and lamented that he was not able to write frequently as there were no stamps to post his letters. He mentioned in this same letter that people were not educated, so they still believed in superstitions.

He also mentioned in his letter that he went to the Kuki expedition after returning from France.

J.P. Mills (1922:19) documented that the "Lhotas are reserved and do not readily open their hearts to a stranger." He further described that "the villagers are swarming with pigs, dogs and cattle. Sanitary arrangement is non-existent" (1922:23). In the early days, polygamy was also practiced. According to J.P. Mills (1922:31), "A well-to-do Lhota usually possesses three wives. The main building of his house therefore contains three sleeping cubicles and a little store room at the back. The front room is occupied by the third wife. The middle room is taken by the chief wife. The back cubicle is used by the second wife."

During those days, the people depended on agriculture for their sustenance. Each family would sow rice, pumpkins, cucumbers, millet, yams, beans, greens, and so on and live on what they harvested. They also reared livestock such as pigs, cows, and chickens. Fish, crabs, and other edibles were harvested from the rivers, as well as wild herbs from the jungle.

In an era where polygamy was the norm, rice beer was used as a food, and people followed a primitive lifestyle in every segment of their lives, anyone showing up and preaching against their way of life faced an uphill battle. The resentment from the villagers did not stop Shanjamo and the early church planters and evangelists from teaching the gospel of Jesus.

According to Mr. Kinghen, a prominent citizen of Wokha, Shanjamo gave him his notes, entrusting it to him to be used as a guide for a biography about his life. The late Mr. N.L. Kinghen served as the chairman of the bench court, appointed by Sir C.R. Pawsy, the deputy commissioner of Kohima, in 1946. He served as chairman of the bench court from 1953–1956. Prior to that, Mr. N.L. Kinghen had served as the peshkar (accountant) at Kohima (P.E. Ezung 1992:40). He was later promoted to political assistant to the deputy commissioner (P.E.Ezung 1992:80). Mr. Kinghen retired as the additional deputy commissioner.

Mr. Wosumo Kikon, a neighbor, stated that Shanjamo not only contributed funds for the purchase of the land at Vankhosung for the Mission Center, but he was also instrumental in pioneering the establishment of the Bible school at Vankhosung. He served as one of the teachers and later was assigned to be the caretaker.

In the words of Rev. Howard and Harriet Houston:

> In 1928 Dr. Bailey came to Wokha after many years in Impur. Dr. Bailey bargained with the shrewd Wokha villagers for a piece of land just beyond the village known as the Vankhosung and bought 32 acres, which became known as the Vankhosung Mission Center. On the top of the hill, Dr. Bailey planned to build their home, and he made the *rock retaining walls for the foundation around which he planted small cedar trees. But in a short time, before his dreams were fulfilled, he died of typhoid fever contracted from drinking tea into which unboiled water had been poured. Today the cedar trees are lovely and tall, shading the ball field where the Bible school students play (Houstons 1987:5).

Shanjamo traveled to the Sema, Ao, and Angami tribes, sharing the gospel and evangelizing local people. He was abused emotionally and verbally by his own people for preaching the Word of God fearlessly. In his correspondence to Mr. Cutler after returning from the States, he did not mention his struggles or mistreatment, nor did he indicate whether he was enjoying his stay in the Naga Hills. Instead, he expressed his gratitude to Mr. Cutler for the great experience that he had at Mount Hermon and for the fond and happy memories of his stay in the United States. He once again exhibited tolerance and a strong positive attitude. He acknowledged that the people in the Naga Hills were uneducated and living in darkness without Christ, though instead of passing judgment, he wrote that the local people were highly superstitious. This is a clear indication that he did not take all of the challenges personally. He endured his struggles with grace and forgave those who mistreated him.

I had the privilege of meeting some of the descendants of Shanjamo, who helped me gather information about his life. It was not easy for him to return to his native land, where his own people were still wearing loincloths, some still naked, and a majority of them practicing animism. Christianity was viewed as a foreign religion and was highly despised. His own people ridiculed him because they did not want to hear him talk about Jesus. In spite of this, Shanjamo passionately shared the Word of God with great enthusiasm.

One tale was told about a couple who went to collect firewood. Unfortunately, a big tree fell on the man, and he died instantly. The villagers, due to their practice of animism and as a result of their highly superstitious beliefs, refused to bring the body to the village because the man had died of a natural calamity. Shanjamo went to the jungle and buried him, but because of this act of burial, he was not allowed by the villagers to return. He told the villagers that because Christ died on the cross and forgave our sins, we must also forgive and love one another. The villagers still refused to let him reenter the village and demanded that Shanjamo perform a pagan ritualistic ceremony in order for him to be welcomed back.

He was told to jump over a fire generated by two sticks and two stones. The ritual was interpreted as an action to burn or chase away evil spirits. Pastor Shanjamo had no choice but to practice situational ethics and jump over the fire as he had nowhere to go. This is a perfect example of the superstitions practiced in Nagaland. In spite of the ill treatment received, Shanjamo was a forgiving man and continued spreading the gospel, and because of his ministry, many people came to know Christ.

In another incident, there was a man in the village who despised and ridiculed Shanjamo for preaching the word of God. It so happened that this man became very sick. In spite of the mistreatment he received, Shanjamo went and prayed for him for healing in the name of Jesus. The man was healed from his ailments. He was overjoyed from being healed from his sickness that he decided to worship the living Christ, and, he along with his household became followers of Jesus who healed him.

Rev. Howard and Harriet Houston, who served as missionaries to the Lotha Tribe from 1947 to 1953, confirmed that "Wokha Mountain is the center of the non-Christian animistic religion. In the caves of the mountain is the land of the dead where the Lothas believe they all go after death. Six bracelets for the men and five bracelets for the women are all that is required to show to the 'great mother' at the entrance of that misty land" (Houstons 1987:2).

As the Houstons left the Wokha Hills for good, their prayer was "Someday, we pray that those large villages around the mountain will be freed from the binding chains of fear and superstition and will yield to the call of Christ. Then the mountain will stand serene, sheltering Christian villages whose people trust in the Rock of Ages" (Houstons 1987:3). V. Nienu also confirmed that "Nagas' relationships with the supernatural were based on animistic practices and were both individual and collective—with a medium for the individual and a priest for the collective community" (Nienu 2015:164). The prayer of Rev. Howard and Harriet Houston was answered. Today the mountains still stand serene and majestic, while the villagers worship the risen Christ, the Rock of Ages.

Mr. P.E. Ezung, another prominent citizen of Wokha Town, gave us a glimpse of Shanjamo's character. Mr. P.E. Ezung was one of the first Christians from Yonchucho Village. He went to Jorhat and graduated from the Agriculture Training Institute, Barpeda Assam, later becoming an elected member of interim body member, the first government established in Nagaland, now known as *member of legislative assembly*. He served as the peace chairman for many years, bringing unity between the underground members and the government of India and participating in negotiations for Naga independence with the Prime Minister of India. He represented Nagas as a member of the delegation team to New Delhi and ultimately obtained the statehood of Nagaland.

Mr. P.E Ezung, this incredible and influential man, is my father. When I was a young girl, he instilled in me the love of Jesus, as well as respect for the many missionaries who traveled to evangelize Nagaland. He held Shanjamo Jungi in highest regard and in his writings gave Shanjamo credit for his contribution to the Naga people. According to my father, Shanjamo was not only an evangelist, but a true patriot and a great leader who led the Naga Labour Corps in France during World War I.

Mr. P.E. Ezung documented that:

In 1927, an American medical missionary, Dr. Bailey took permission from the SDO Mokokchung, Mr. J.P. Mills, to open the Lotha Mission Centre at Vankosung. Through this mission school in Vankosung, there was an increase in education among the Lothas (Kyongs). The land was purchased from the Wokha Village people. The students were: Luke Kikon, Ekyimo Ngully (Okotso Village); Phandeo Ngully (Okotso Village); Abraham, Tssenchio Kikon, Nlŭmo Murry, (Okotso Village) and Nzio Hŭmtsoe (Tsungiki Village). The teachers were: Chŭmdemo Murry (Okotso Village); Subongsuba Ao, Shanchamo Jungi (Yikhum Village) (Ezung 1992:34).

In spite of his many contributions as a preacher, teacher, choir leader, and veteran of the First World War, Shanjamo remained humble and continued to teach and preach the gospel of Jesus Christ. When I interviewed his only surviving son, Mr. Yanrenthung, I asked him to give me a glimpse of the life of his father. His answer was that his father Shanjamo would preach the Word of God, but his words often fell on deaf ears. People did not want to hear his teachings or sermons and would often laugh at him. With tears in his eyes, Mr. Yanrenthung told me that his beloved father would cry, watching people leave in the middle of his sermons. He would often arrive early to church, before the ringing of the church bells, eager to share the Word of God with any who would open their hearts to listen.

Because Shanjamo was well-educated, it could be that his teachings weren't understood by the local villagers. Working with uneducated individuals brought many challenges, but he was not deterred. As a graduate of Mt. Hermon Boys School, he exhibited academic excellence, dedication, and passion in evangelism. It is likely that it was challenging and confusing for the natives to comprehend any teachings from someone who had been educated at such a prestigious institution, especially in an era when superstition was highly regarded.

The early Naga Christians suffered verbal and emotional abuse from the non-Christians all over the Naga Hills. They were often harassed and their lives threatened.

Shanjamo was ahead of his time due to his advanced education in the United States; he was misunderstood by the local people in Nagaland. A hundred years ago, it must have been difficult to change one's belief from the ancestral worship of animism to Christianity. As a real enthusiast for the gospel of Jesus Christ, Shanjamo truly understood the plan of salvation, though the local people were not able to readily accept the Christian faith.

However, all was not lost. As a result of his passionate work, along with that of the many dedicated missionaries and faithful Christians, Nagaland has been proclaimed to be a Christian state today. It is difficult to know exactly how many Nagas are faithful followers of Jesus Christ, since Nagaland, like anywhere, is plagued with corruption, but there are sincere believers who faithfully and joyfully serve the living Christ.

A farewell letter written to the Houstons on behalf of the Lotha Tribe by the chairman of the Lotha tribal bench, Wokha, describes the ministry of Shanjamo as follows: "In 1910 there were a few converts in Okotso Village for the second time, and Mr. Shanjamo, who went to America in 1904 and returned in 1908, and who was working with Mr. R.B. Longwell in Impur was sent to Okotso for a short time to be the helper of the pastor of that church. Thus the real mission work in the Lotha country started in 1910 and churches were re-organized" (Houstons 1987:57).

Rev. Longwell and his wife served the Ao and Lotha Tribes from 1906 through 1927. Shanjamo worked closely with the Longwells, assisting them in interpretations and partnering with them in ministry work. I had the privilege of meeting Robert Doll, the grandson of Rev. R.B Longwell, and his wife, Judy Dole. Both are retired ministers of God, currently living in Vancouver, British Columbia, Canada.

In a letter written by Rev. Howard Houston on November 1, 1948, he mentioned that "Shanjamo asked for leave this morning to go to his village for two months." It indicates that Shanjamo worked closely with the Houstons. Having lived in America himself, Shanjamo could relate well with the Houstons, sharing memories and reflecting on American culture.

Rev. Bengt Anderson mentioned that he went to Littami Village in the Sema Naga Tribe. He was surprised to find Shanjamo pastoring and teaching there. In the words of Rev. Bengt Anderson: "We descended some five miles, crossed a turbulent Doyang river, yes it has a bridge, and climbed perhaps only four miles, but we were satisfied when the happy Semas came part of the way to meet us. Here we had surprises: one was to meet a village teacher who spoke English. His name was Shanjamo and he had been to America, sponsored by an American Baptist Missionary years before" (Anderson 1978:12).

Vankhosung Mission Center still stands, and the ministry continues. Due to the generous giving of Dr. Bailey, Shanjamo, and the others who contributed, Vankhosung Mission Center is home to many ministers of God, a Bible college, and a small mission hospital. The Houstons remarked that: "The Lotha Christians look up to Vankhosung as a lighthouse from where the light of the Gospel will shed its saving rays upon all the Lotha villages. The churches sent their young people to the Bible school and women's training school with great confidence and hope in us that we would train them well in God's Word and Christian customs" (Houston's 1987:34).

The Houstons taught at Vankhosung Bible School from 1947 through 1953, and Rev. Houston traveled to villages, sharing the gospel of Jesus Christ. However, they were not allowed to return to Nagaland by the Indian government after their furlough to the United States. After Nagaland, they served in the Philippines for many years and then retired at the Claremont Retirement Home in Southern California. They have four children: Frank, Carol, Jan, and Steve. Frank and Carol were born in Jorhat, Assam. The Lothas gave them Lotha names. Frank's Lotha name is Mhathung which means "born in a time of blessing." Carol's Lotha name is Mhabeni which means "fulfillment of blessings."

The Houstons built a home in Vankhosung, and the house, although in disrepair, still stands today, serving as the residence of the field director of the mission. Mrs. Houston describes the building of their home in this way:

During the time we were in Kohima, Howard built a house for us in Vankhosung. A missionary has to be a jack of all trades. Before the house was built, he bought about a dozen enormous trees in the forest reserve—some for Rs. 5 (51) and some for Rs.10 (12) each. These were felled and sawed into boards out in the jungle. The sawyers, four pair of them, worked on a platform. One man above the platform pulled the saw up and one man below the platform pulled the saw down until the boards were all cut. Then village men dragged the boards three miles to Vankhosung, where they were piled to dry while the foundations were hewn out of the mountainside. Just below the site for the house there was good rock, but the Wokha Village stone cutters, non-Christians, were afraid to cut it because it was the "devil's cooking pot," they believe. So stones for the foundations were cut a mile away and hauled over in the jeep. The sand was carried up on the backs of men and women from a river five miles below Vankhosung. Howard took in two Angami carpenters from Kohima to build the house, who, along with Lotha carpenters and helpers, finished it in little more than six months. Every board was planed by hand, and all the tools used were very simple. The house was 24 x 24, with two small bedrooms, a living-dining room, bath, kitchen, storeroom and an office for Howard. The unfinished upstairs was used for clothes drying and storage, and at one end we fixed up an extra bedroom (Houstons 1987:47).

In the introduction to the book *The Lotha Nagas*, by J.P. Mills, Mr. J.H. Hutton wrote:

One of the first disputes I had to settle when I went to Mokokchung in 1913 was a complaint from the village of Pangti that a missionary had been initiating his converts by immersing them in the village spring, to which the village elders objected both on sanitary and religious (or, if you will, superstitious) grounds. According to the elders, 'they wash their nasty sins in my pool, and it poisoned the cow' (Mills 1992: xi).

Mr. Mills served as the sub-divisional officer in Mokokchung in the 1920s, while Mr. J.H. Hutton served as the deputy commissioner of the Naga Hills and the director of ethnography in Assam.

Mr. Hutton noted:

At Okotso, a third of the village had turned Christian: the re-mainder, having observed that no immediate disaster seemed to follow the forsaking of ancestral customs, but being in no wise desirous to take up the burden of the angel of the Church of Impur, who looks with disapproval on tobacco and the na-tional dress and insists on total prohibition as regards fer-mented liquor, had lapsed into a spiritual limbo in which they observed no religious customs at all (Mills 1922: xii).

Perhaps the resistance to the gospel is due to a strong devotion to long-held customs. The fermented liquor, also known as rice beer, is a local delicacy to the Nagas. It is a cultural recipe passed down through generations. This local brew is considered a health supplement and a common part of their diet. In addition, it was a way of life, consumed at gatherings and celebrations. To be told to give up this drink meant rejecting long-standing social traditions and likely would have been met with skepticism and resistance.

Growing up in Nagaland in a Baptist Christian home, I heard about rice beer. As a young girl, we were told that only non-Christians consumed it and other alcoholic beverages. We were not even allowed to taste it, as it was forbidden for Christians to partake. People who drank wine and other forms of alcohol were regarded as sinners and ex-communicated from church membership.

Even to this day, Baptist churches impose total prohibition of al-coholic sales in Nagaland. As a result, there are many closet drinkers, and some travel to the neighboring state of Assam to drink, boosting their economy instead of helping the local economy. Nagaland is a dry state by declaration, but alcohol abuse is still rampant among the local population. Naga Christians still observe and respect ancient traditional practices, and many remain highly superstitious. Shanjamo and the early Christians encountered many of these conflicts during their ministries, but they kept their faith and focused on their commitment to God.

Many forms of old superstitions are still practiced to this day. In towns and cities, people are slowly assimilating, but in villages, the locals (including Christians) follow and carry out superstitious beliefs passed down from their ancestors.

Shanjamo could have obtained a secular job as he was close to several British officials, including Mr. J.P. Mills and Dr. J.H. Hutton. But he remained faithful to God and tirelessly shared the gospel of Jesus Christ. Dr. Clark was still at Impur when Shanjamo returned home to Nagaland, and it must have been quite a blessed reunion for them, as well as for the Houstons at Vankhosung. Shanjamo was a direct product of the mission work of the American Baptist missionaries and a first generation Christian who passionately evangelized the Nagas.

On February 18, 1973, in a speech during the Golden Jubilee at Wokha Baptist Church, N.L. Kinghen remarked that Shanjamo had declared openly and publicly: "I have decided never to touch any institutional work, and I feel that God has called me to pioneer evangelism." In Mr. Kinghen's words: "Late Mr. Jungi was once asked by Dr. J.H. Hutton, the then deputy commissioner, Naga Hills, whether he would like to go to the medical school at Dibrugarh, and his reply was, 'Thank you very much, sir, for offering me a better chance, but as for me, I have already chosen to serve the Lord, and that is my last choice.'"

Mr. Kinghen also confirmed that sometime in the middle part of 1924, Mr. J.P. Mills, the sub-divisional officer in Mokokchung, fell ill, and Dr. James R. Bailey, the medical missionary at Impur, was notified. Dr. Bailey took care of Mr. Mills, who was suffering from double pneumonia as well as other complications. His illness was so serious that Dr. Bailey stayed at Mokokchung to provide the best care. Eventually, Mr. Mills recovered from his sickness and gratefully offered to pay Dr. Bailey for his service, but Dr. Bailey declined. Instead, Dr. Bailey requested to grant him a piece of land at Wokha. Mr. J.P. Mills gladly granted permission as a token of his gratitude, and the Vankhosung Mission Field started in 1925. Dr. Bailey and Shanjamo paid for the cost of the land.

Dr. Bailey went to Calcutta to purchase the supplies needed for construction at the new mission center. Sadly, he was stricken with typhoid and died in Calcutta at the age of 51. His death was a devastating setback for the Lotha Nagas. Rev. Bengt Anderson mentioned that Mrs. Bailey was willing to stay and continue the ministry among the Lotha Naga Tribe, but she was discouraged from doing so, as she had five children in the US who needed her more than the Nagas did (Anderson 1978:28).

Dr. Bailey's death was unexpected and a shock to his friends and family. Dr. R.B. Longwell, in his eulogy "An Appreciation," wrote that Dr. Bailey loved the Nagas and always had the interest of the Nagas at heart. According to Rev. Longwell, Dr. Bailey, during his first furlough during World War I, had traveled to France to assist the Nagas who were there as the Naga Labour Corps under the leadership of Shanjamo. For Dr. Bailey to sacrifice his furlough and instead serve the Nagas who were in France during the war shows a beautiful testament of his compassion, love, and dedication to the Naga people. It also shows that Shanjamo and Dr. Bailey shared a strong bond of friendship and for the service of the Lord. I can only imagine the joy on the faces of the Nagas upon seeing Dr. Bailey again in France. It must have been a wonderful and joyful reunion for both Dr. Bailey and the Nagas.

While researching about the life of Shanjamo, my heart was touched to realize how much he and the early Christians endured while sharing Christ in those primitive days. It was truly a spiritual warfare, a critical time of crossroads, yet we see the power of God prevailing in victory. My heart is comforted by knowing that Evangelist Shanjamo and the early Christians received tremendous emotional support from the American Baptist Missionaries. Having the support of our friends and family as we go through our own challenges and struggles of life is wonderful. We also need our friends and family to celebrate with us in our triumphs. I am blessed to know that the early Christians also had the support of their friends and loved ones. The American Baptist missionaries, on the other hand, saw their ministry carried on by the local Christian leaders whom they had trained—a real blessing and a powerful testimony to see God at work and the power of the mighty God we serve.

To all these warriors of our Lord Jesus, we give our heartfelt gratitude for their obedience to our Lord Jesus.

The Lord has welcomed home Shanjamo and the early Christians, saying, *"thou good and faithful servant… enter thou into the joy of thy Lord"* (Matthew 25:21, KJV).

Rev. Howard and Harriet Houston, carrying Carol Rose (Mhabeni) on Howard's back Naga style. The Houstons were missionaries to the Lotha Tribe in Naga Hills, 1947–1953. (Photo: Courtesy Rev. and Mrs. Houston)

Welcome gate at Vankhosung Mission Center (Lotha Tribe) as it is today

Vankhosung Mission Center, Wokha Nagaland, as it is today.
Dr. Bailey and Shanjamo purchased 32 acres of land

Changtongya Baptist
Church, as it is today (Ao
Tribe). Pastor Shanjamo
served as the pastor from
1909–1910

Changtongya Village (Ao Tribe), Nagaland.

Shanjamo was sent to Okotso Village by
Rev. R.B. Longwell to assist the pastor of
Okotso Baptist Church around 1910–1911.

"In 1910 there were a few converts
in Okotso Village for the second time, and
Mr. Shanjamo, who went to America in 1904
and returned in 1908 and who was working
with Mr. R.B. Longwell in Impur, was sent to
Okotso for a short time to be the helper of the
pastor of that church. Thus, the real mission
work in the Lotha country started in 1910,
and churches were re-organized" (Houstons
1987:57).

Okotso Village

Changbang Baptist Church (Lotha Tribe), where Pastor Shanjamo served as Pastor from 1912–1913

Yikhum Baptist Church (Lotha Tribe) (newly constructed)

Yikhum Village, Pastor Shanjamo's Village. Pastor Shanjamo served as the pastor in 1914. Again served as the pastor from 1919–1920

Old Changsu Baptist Church
(Lotha Tribe) (newly constructed)

Old Changsu Village,
the village where Pastor
Shanjamo Jungi served as
pastor from 1921–1922

Old Littami Baptist Church (Sema Tribe) (newly constructed)

Old Littami Village, Nagaland. Pastor Shanjamo Jungi
served as the first pastor from 1927–1929

Shanjamo's Family Life

S HANJAMO MARRIED AN Ao lady named Noksanglemla Lemur, of Longpa Village on Sunday, April 11, 1909 (Kinghen 1972:15). They did not have any children. During those days, communication with loved ones was often not possible since no internet, cell phones, telephones, or other means of communication existed. Shanjamo left for France on March 1, 1917, with the Naga Labour Corps and did not return to Kohima, Naga Hills, until June 17, 1918. As a result, when Shanjamo left for the war, his wife left for her village for the simple reason that Shanjamo might not return from the war (Kinghen 1972:16). Upon his return, Shanjamo went to his wife's village to bring her home. Unfortunately, he discovered that she had already remarried.

During the war, a young Lotha man, Thezamo, of Pangti Village had been killed. One of his friends from Pangti Village wrote a song in commemoration:

Pangti khyongroe Thezamo
(Thezamo, young man of Pangti Village)
Etsu Thawa lo rocho (he came to fight in the French war)
Heto Yipa Vanato (Why you are sleeping like this)
Nra panthi etsoyo tsosi (Please get up and eat your meal)
Ete elhi lo wotavkalo (Let us go and fulfill our duty)

This beautiful poem was sung to me by Mr. Wosumo Kikon of Yikhum Village; he was 103 years of age when I met and interviewed him in July of 2016.

After the death of Thezamo, his comrades sang this song with so much pain and sheer sadness as they missed their friend and fellow soldier. However, the British commanders discouraged their singing because it left people feeling brokenhearted, and there was concern it would affect morale. A ban on singing of the song was instated, and those who disobeyed were fined Rs.500. Because this was an astronomical sum of money at that time, Thezamo's fellow comrades fell silent. Thezamo was laid to rest in Germany.

Mr. P.E. Ezung confirms the details of Shanjamo's enlistment and service:

The First World War started from Germany in Europe and lasted four years (1914–1918). Altogether 400 Lothas (Kyong) men participated in the First World War under the leadership of Mr. Shanchamo Jungi; he was the head man or the person in charge of the corps; [he]…was from Yikhum village. He had returned from his study in America. This was another occasion to earn some money by the Lotha (Kyong) Labour Corps. This resulted in the introduction of the use of currency, which brought prosperity and economic uplift among the people (P.E. Ezung 1992:32–33).

Shanjamo's adopted son, Mr. Yanrenthung, told me that his dad brought back many coins from the war. Shanjamo would drop the coins into a winnowing bamboo basket and count them. The Naga Labour Corps members were paid for their service, helping the local economy flourish. We can rightfully say that Shanjamo was instrumental in improving the economy and bringing prosperity in the land.

Upon Shanjamo's return after the war, Shanjamo met and married a Lotha girl by the name Chomoni from Riphym Village in 1919. She was the aunt of the former honorable minister, the late Mr. N.L. Odyuo. Mr. Odyuo's father and Chomoni were siblings. Since Shanjamo and Chomoni did not have children of their own, they adopted three children:

Mr. Sathungo Jungi of Juti Village, who was given the name Moses,
Ms. Sumlamvu from Old Riphym, and
Mr. Yanrenthung from Old Riphym.

Mr. Sathungo's Story

Sathungo Moses was married and had one son. During my visit to the village, I stopped by and met Sathungo's son and his wife. Sathungo's son was ill at the time and unfortunately couldn't communicate well. On the other hand, his wife was very cheerful and articulate, and we exchanged warm greetings. Rev. Howard Houston, in a letter to his wife Harriet Houston, wrote from Yikhum Village on March 17: "I met Mosa, Shanjamo's son, who is becoming a fine-looking young man."

Ms. Sumlamvu's Story

Sumlamvu never married, and she took the responsibility of caring for her father in his later years until his death. Shortly before he died, Shanjamo told his daughter Sumlamvu that his days on earth were numbered, and he prayed that God would take him home before disaster struck. Soon after his death on February 28, 1956, the Indian Army came and burned the entire Yikhum Village on July 29, 1956.

Yanrenthung's Account

Shanjamo's two adopted children listed above have already died. However, after my visit to Yikhum Village, I learned that Shanjamo's youngest son was still alive and residing with his son at Wokha Town. I immediately jumped at the opportunity to interview him in person.

It was a hot and humid summer day when I arrived in Wokha Town, and navigating was difficult as there are no street signs or house numbers. We asked locals for help in locating Yanrenthung's home and eventually found the general area where he lived. The jeep we were driving soon became of no use due to deteriorating road conditions.

My sister, Nkonbeni Ezung, had accompanied me, and on foot we hiked up the uneven terrain of the rough, unpaved hill, which led to Mr. Yanrenthung's house.

I was excited to meet the youngest son of Shanjamo's three adopted children. Yanrenthung was well-dressed and seated on a chair basking in the sun. He was very soft-spoken, quiet, gentle, and calm as I introduced myself and asked for his permission to obtain more information about his parents. Initially he was very reserved, but after a while, he became comfortable and talked openly about his relationship with his parents, whom he loved deeply. According to Yanrenthung, his parents were kind, thoughtful, and committed to the well-being of their children.

When I asked him to relay memories of his dad, he shared that he often accompanied him on preaching tours. His dad, a highly devoted Christian, would preach tirelessly about the love of Jesus. He remembered his dad's shedding tears when people, obviously yet to be convicted as sinners in need of God's love and forgiveness, left the service in the middle of a sermon. No matter the obstacles, his dad had continued to preach the plan of salvation and the forgiveness of Jesus. He carried out his ministry work with joy and passion. At times he was hurt, sad, brokenhearted, and discouraged, but these obstacles didn't stop him from sharing the gospel of Jesus Christ to eager listeners.

Shanjamo's desire to be a missionary was grounded in his belief that the local villagers were heathen and living in a culture of superstition. In his application to Mount Hermon School, he had noted that his desire was to return to the Naga Hills and share the salvation of Jesus. Mr. Yanrenthung confirmed how hard his father had worked to fulfill this purpose, dedicated to serving Christ even in the midst of adversities, discouragement, and disappointment.

Mr. Yanrenthung repeatedly affirmed that he felt loved by his adoptive parents. The fact that Shanjamo and Chomoni took in orphaned children as their own, offering them a nurturing and devoted home, speaks volumes to their compassionate and loving hearts.

According to Mr. Yanrenthung, during the Second World War, the British worked closely with Shanjamo because he had been educated abroad and spoke English well. Yanrenthung also recounted his memories of the British officials staying at their place at Yikhum Village.

When I asked Mr. Yanrenthung what he would like to say to his dad when he sees him in heaven, he became emotional, pausing as the tears welled up in his eyes. After he paused, he drew in a long breath and responded: "I will thank my father for loving me very much and would tell him how happy I am to see him again."

Mr. Yanrenthung sang in the Yikhum Baptist choir and served as the caretaker of the church for many years. He was living with his son, daughter-in-law, and grandchildren in Wokha. He was approximately 80 years of age at the time of the interview in July of 2016. During my visit in July of 2019, I learned that he went home to be with the Lord in February of 2019.

Shanjamo and Chomoni also took in another girl by the name Ms. Ntseno and raised her as their own after her parents died.

I had the privilege of meeting the daughters of Ntseno, Mrs. Loreni and Mrs. Lovungi. Both daughters currently live in Dimapur, Nagaland with their families. Loreni and Lovungi joyfully shared memories about their grandfather, which had been passed down from their mom.

Shanjamo led the Naga labour Corps during the First World War

According to them, their grandfather's house was used as the Grand Central Station of communications by the British during the World War II, and the soldiers would often share food and other supplies during their stay at Yikhum Village. According to their mom, their grandparents truly loved all of their children.

Medals awarded during First World war.
Shanjamo was awarded some of these medals.

Shanjamo Memorial Baptist High School

THE EXECUTIVE MEMBERS of the Lotha Baptist Association met on November 22, 1968, and after a thorough discussion, the committee decided to name the Baptist English School in Wokha Town in honor of Shanjamo's contributions in evangelizing the Naga people, the Lothas in particular. The Shanjamo Memorial Baptist English School was one of the two Christian private schools in those days. The other private institution was the Catholic Don Bosco School.

I was a student at the Shanjamo Memorial Baptist English School for several years. The school was fully enrolled and well attended at that time. The principal of the school, Mr. David Mangrati, along with his wife, came from Darjeeling to spend many years serving along with Mr. and Mrs. Barrows. The school continues to serve children in the community, and my prayer is that it will continue to thrive and produce many contributing leaders, serving Jesus as their Lord and making Him the center of their lives.

At present, the school is run by a board of directors from Wokha Village.

"The elders who direct the affairs of the church well are worthy of double honor, especially those whose work is preaching and teaching" (1 Timothy 5:17).

Shanjamo Memorial Baptist English School Wokha, Nagaland

Wokha Town where Shanjamo Memorial Baptist
High School is located at the bottom of the picture.

◇◇◇◇◇◇◇◇◇◇◇

Collection of Letters and Forms

(Courtesy of Northfield Mount Hermon Archives)

Port Norris
New Jersey

October 13, 1906

To the Superintendent of the Mount Hermon Boys School

My dear sir:

Mr. Perrine and I brought home with us from Assam a Naga boy from the Naga Hills who is at present attending public school here.

Last week at a missionary meeting in Newark, I met Mrs. Albert G. Ropes of Morristown New Jersey, who has offered to send our boy to the Mount Hermon School. Will you kindly send to my address a curriculum and any other information which may be valuable in entering a pupil in your school. Sanchamo is about nineteen years old and is in the eighth grade at school. This is his second year only in this country, but he understands English very well I think. I hope he may be able to enter soon at Northfield.

Respectfully yours,

Mrs. R.L Perrine
(Rose Lamb Perrine)

(Actual Document Replicated)

American Baptist Missionary Union, Accredited Representative
Rev. Samuel Alden Perrine. Ten Years Missionary in Assam, India

Address: Port Norris, New Jersey

November 26, 1906

My Dear Irene Ropes,

No doubt you have wondered whether you were ever to hear from
me again or no. But you must remember that we are living in
South Jersey now, and next to Assam, South Jersey is the slowest
place I know of. We have not forgotten you nor your kind offer on
behalf of Sanchamo, and I have only been waiting that I might have
something definite to say when I did write.

The catalogue of the Mt. Hermon School is before me, and as I
look over the entrance examinations of September 1905, I fear
that Sanchamo will not be able to pass these exams at the end of
this school year. That is unless they are somewhat lenient towards
foreigners, and yet the principal of his school here has known of
boys who have been received in the Mt. Hermon School, who were
no further advanced then Sanchamo is now.

Sanchamo is in the seventh grade now but should be able to
complete the eighth before entering at Northfield. He would then
have had no physics; questions in which are given under the head of
elementary science. He has physiology this year and in arithmetic
will go three denominate numbers.

As far as the other studies are concerned, I think he would be able
to cope with them unless it was grammar; he would no doubt be a
little lame there.

In June he will have been in this country two years, and I think it
advisable that he get there as soon as possible, so I would like him

to get started in Northfield as soon as they will take him. Have they any preparatory work, do you know? If he would have instruction during the Summer I think, he would be able to enter next September. In any case he would like to continue his studies during the Summer (School here closes in May).

They also sent me a medical certificate which I shall have filled out in a few days.

Now there is nothing at all definite about this; perhaps you who know Mt. Hermon School better than I can see something in it upon which to plan. I leave it with you to suggest, and we will try to follow out your suggestions as early as possible. Although I hate to send the dear boy away, yet for his good I am willing to let him go as it can be arranged.

You spoke about a photograph; there is no place here to get one. On December 11, he goes with me to Millville to speak, and I think he will be able to get one taken while there.

Trusting that you are well and that this Thanksgiving season may be a happy one to you. I remain.

Very cordially yours,

Mrs. R.L. Perrine and Mr. S. A. Perrine

(Actual Document Replicated)

The Northfield Schools
D.L. Moody, Founder
Office of the Secretary
East Northfield Mass

January 1, 1907

Mr. H. F. Cutler, Mass

Dear Mr. Cutler:

I am enclosing two letters which I would ask you to kindly acknowledge.

The one from Mrs. Ropes I have acknowledged by saying that in general we do not advise students coming from foreign lands as Missionary Boards are maintaining at great expense education institutions. I do not at all know how she will take it, but I have said that you will write her, and possibly may be able to find room for the boy during the summer term.

To Mr. Day, I have replied that I am sending the information he requests and referring his letter to you.

With best wishes for a happy New Year, believe me.

Yours sincerely,

W.R. Moody

(Actual Document Replicated)

Port Norris, New Jersey

January 7, 1907

My Dear Mrs. Ropes,

Your letter together with Mr. Moody's [was] received on Saturday. His attitude is not surprising, and ordinarily his inferences would be wholly correct. I can see how in many cases his objections would be valid. But we missionaries at Impur considered the question carefully, weighing each one of these objections before starting to America: and it seemed best to us to bring Sanchamo to America for his preparations. Dr. E. A. Clark now nearly thirty-eight years in Assam approved the plan heartily and forwarded the expense of his voyage here. We have tried the other plan, that of educating our teachers in India and for us it has proved a failure. Our situation and needs are perhaps peculiar and our Nagas are different from the plains people. The environment any place in India outside of Assam would be almost as foreign to a Naga as America is. We hope soon to have this supplied in Assam; then our teachers can be prepared there.

At present, Sanchamo knows nothing about Hinduism or caste and it would be quite impossible to send him anywhere in India but what he would imitate many false ideas, which we are trying to keep out of our field and which are prevalent in most parts of India. The winters at Northfield had already been considered by me. But I believe he will be able to stand them just as well as he has this damp chill of New Jersey the past two winters. Our hill people are accustomed to cold, going wholly unprotected with mercury at 4.5 sometimes while they know nothing of the intense heat of India. I do hope that the objectives [whole sentence not clear] will not interfere with your sending Sanchamo to Northfield for a trial at least. If after they have given him a fair trial, he does not seem to be benefited, why of course we would consider it our duty to place him elsewhere or send him back.

His medical form has been filled out. Shall I send it to you? Thank you for the beautiful Thot's in your former letter. I do indeed pray that you and we may be guided in this, to me [and] to him, very important matter. If Sanchamo knew I was writing, he would wish to send his Salaams.

Very sincerely yours,

R.L. Perrine (Mrs. Rose Ermina Perrine)

(Actual Document Replicated)

Port Norris

New Jersey

January 24th, 1907

Mr. Henry F. Cutler:

My dear sir—I am sending the application to the Mt. Hermon School on behalf of Sanchamo, our Naga boy. I trust that he will be able to enter in May as his school here closes in May and I want to keep him busy during the Summer. However, I am not particular about his taking a full time of studies for the Summer term. If he could begin a systematic system of study of the Bible and take something to increase his knowledge of English, I should consider that enough with hope, that is, if you could keep him busy out of doors for the rest of the time. I would like him to see for instance how pigs are cared for in a civilized country and some garden work. I think it will be good for him. However, he should be getting English as fast as possible and Bible study place above all studies. It is our hope that he will be able to teach any Grammar school studies when he returns to Assam.

I hope you will not call him John or any other name in place of his own. Just remember a-ah and San-cha-mo is not difficult to pronounce.

Sincerely yours,

R.L. Perrine

(Actual Document Replicated)

January 26, 1907

Name of Candidate: *Sanchamo*

Address: *Port Norris, New Jersey*

Date of birth: *About March 1887*

Date of filling out this blank: *January 24, 1907*

When does he wish to enter: *Beginning Summer Term 1907*

What form does he hope to enter? *Left for your decision.*

Does he apply for the full course? *Not necessarily*

If not how long does he intend to remain? *As long as seems wise*

Name and address of person filling out this blank: *Mrs. R.L. Perrine, Port Norris, New Jersey*

Name and address of parent/guardian? *Rev. S.A. Perrine, Port Norris, New Jersey*

Please fill out the above blanks.

1. Name in full of candidate for admission. *Sanchamo*

2. Birthplace. *Yikhum. Naga Hills, Assam, India*

3. Send a physician's certificate to health (blank enclosed)

4. Has candidate done anything toward self-support? *Yes*
   In what occupation? *General work about the house and garden*

5. What schools attended and how long? *Impur Mission six years. Trenton Junctions and Port Norris Public, 1 year each.*

6. Amount of work done in the following studies, giving rank if possible.
   Arithmetic. Standard Arith. Denominate No Ave 86
   Grammar and Analysis. Etymology—verbs
   Geography. He has practically finished the large geography
   U.S. History. Now in advance administration War of 1812

7. If higher branches have been studied, state amount of work done in each. *This year taking Physiology. Now studying nervous system.*

8. Any market preference in study, reading and occupation?
   Fond of reading and study, especially the Bible

9. Has candidate shown an ambition to excel in anything?
   Bible Teaching

10. Has he formed any purpose in life? *To be an Apostle to his people*

11. What prominent traits of character?

    Truthfulness
    Conscientiousness
    Faithfulness

11. Has he had any bad companionship? *Not since he has come to the mission when he was about twelve years of age.*

13. Does he use tobacco? *No.* Has he any bad habits? *No*

14. Is he a member of any church? *Impur Baptist Church. Naga Hills, Assam.*

15. In what religious belief educated? *Baptist*

16. If not a member of a church, has he shown any interest in religion?

17. Why do you wish to send him to this school? *To prepare him for a teacher among his people in Assam.*

18. Does the candidate himself wish to come here? *Yes*

19. Full names and addresses of father, mother, guardian or nearest friend? *Rev. S.A. Perrine. Pastor of the Port Norris Baptist Church*

20. Are they in church membership?

21. Their occupation? Can they afford to send the applicant to a more expensive school? *No*

22. Who will be responsible for the pupil's board and tuition? *Mrs. Albert G. Ropes. Morristown, New Jersey*

23. Who will be responsible for other expenses? *Mrs. Ropes*

24. Send names and addresses of the following?

    Pastor? *Rev. S.A. Perrine*

    Last Employer (or some business man)

    Last Teacher: *Miss E. Stambaugh, Port Norris, New Jersey*

(Actual Document Replicated)

Port Norris, NJ

1/30/07

Henry Cutler MD
Mount Hermon Mass

My dear Sir:

It gives me pleasure to recommend Sanchamo to you as a candidate for admission to your school. He has been my pupil this year, and I have found him to be an honest, conscientious boy and very easily disciplined. He is in the eighth grade and possesses a fair knowledge of U.S. History, Arithmetic, Geography, Grammar, Spelling, Physiology, etc.

Sanchamo is a close student, is very eager to learn, and has no difficulty in grasping any new idea or subject presented to him.

He seems to have mastered the English language remarkably well and is especially good in Spelling, Reading and Grammar. He frequently has difficulty in finding words to express himself— seems to understand but cannot tell his thoughts.

Trusting that I have been explicit enough, I am

Respectfully,

Elda G. Stambaugh

(Elda G. Stambaugh was the principal of Port Norris Public School)

(Actual Document Replicated)

Port Norris, New Jersey

February 4, 1907

Mr. Cutter,

I so anxiously desire to attend your school, because our Lord brought me here to get a better education and to do His will, so I can serve Him better when I go to my homeland.

He loves me so much so He has chosen me from among my people. Among my people there are only three teachers to teach them so they want more teachers to teach them, because they have never heard the gospel of Jesus. I hope I will be able to teach them when I go back to my homeland so please pray for me always.

Yours Sincerely,

Sanchamo Christian

(Actual Document Replicated)

American Baptist Missionary Union
Accredited Representative
Rev. Samuel Alden Perrine
Port Norris, New Jersey

March 18, 1907

Mr. H.F. Cutler:
Mount Hermon
Massachusetts

My dear sir:

I am writing to say that you can certainly expect Sanchamo to begin the Spring term with you on May 3 and he will arrive on May 2 as you suggest.

It is desired that he enter from school certificates from the schools here so will you kindly send the necessary certificate forms.

Thanking you for all good offices to him.

Yours most sincerely,

S.A. Perrine

(Actual Document Replicated)

Application for Admission

To

Mount Hermon School

Mount Hermon, Massachusetts

Applicants will understand that filling out this blank does not imply the acceptance of the candidate.

Every application will be considered on its own merits, and its relation to other applications, existing vacancies, and the purpose of the school. Meritorious cases maybe refused because they do not fall in line with the special design of the school or because others have a prior claim.

Applicants are requested to answer every question with equal care and candor. Flattering or misleading statements regarding the mental or moral character of the candidate may bring about his admission to the school, but will only act against him when he is here seen and known.

Among the indispensable conditions of admissions are a sound mind and a sound body. Feeble minds with no aptitude for study, and feeble bodies with no power of endurance, are excluded, not because they need no help, but because the school is not adapted to this class of pupils. Lazy boys are not desired.

Every accepted candidate is received upon the understanding that he will prove himself worthy of the advantages offered him or consent to forfeit them.

The parent, guardian, or some responsible person will fill out this blank and return to the principal of the school.

Each applicant is requested to send his photograph (small one preferred), and also a letter of his own composition and writing, stating what studies he has pursued, what his purpose in life is, and what course of study he wishes to take here.

(Sample, Duplicated)

Medical Examiner's Certificate
of Candidate for Admission
to the Mount Hermon School

Name of Applicant: *Sanchamo*

Address: *Port Norris, New Jersey*

Nationality: *Lotha, Naga.* Color: *Brown.* Height: *5ft 2¾ in.*
Weight: *110.* Age: *19*

1. How long have you known the applicant personally? *Four months*

2. Does his general appearance indicate good health? *Yes*

3. Has the applicant any physical defects? *No*
   (Any defect that will interfere with the performance of manual labor or with the work of a student should be especially
   mentioned)

4. What are they?

5. Girth of chest under vest, at rest *32* under full inspiration *33* under
   forced expiratio*n 30.*

6. Is the respiration full, easy, regular? *Yes.* Number per minute? *14*
   Murmur normal over every part of both lungs? *Yes*

7. Is there any disease of organs of respiration? *No*

8. Is the action of the heart clear, uniform, rhythmic? *Yes*

9. Is there any disease of the heart or blood vessels? *No*

10. Give rate and character of the pulse, sitting *64,* standing *76*

11. Is there any disease or disorder of stomach, abdominal or pelvic
    organs? *No*

12. Any evidence of successful vaccination? *Yes*

13. Has the applicant a rupture? *No.* If so, how severe?

14. Has the applicant any disease of the nervous system (chorea,
    epilepsy, etc.) *No*
    If so, to what extent?

15. Has the applicant any disease or condition which requires medical attention or special care of any kind? *No*

The foregoing are full and true answers to the questions proposed.

Signed: Stetson L. Bacon, Medical Examiner

Date: November 30th, 1906

Address: Port Norris, New Jersey

A registered medical practitioner according to the laws of: Graduated at the Jeff Medical College. Philadelphia, March 1858

(Actual Document Replicated)

Mount Hermon School

Application for Exemption from Examination

April 5, 1907

I hereby make application for exemption from entrance examination in the subjects indicated below, for which I offer signed certificate of work done.

Signed: Sanchamo

Address of Applicant: Port Norris, New Jersey

This certificate must be filled out and signed by the teacher, principal or superintendent under whom the work is done, and forwarded to

Henry F. Cutler, Mount Hermon. Massachusetts.

Subjects offered for advanced standing maybe added in the blank spaces.

Subject	Text book	Amount	No. of weeks	Periods per week	Rank	Date of Completion
Languages						
English Grammar	Raul's Practical English Grammar	To Syntax	34	5	Very Good	
English Composition	Raul's Etymology		8	5	Very Good	
Latin First Year Math Arithmetic	Brook's Arithmetic	Stocks & Bonds With Percentage	34	5	Good	
Algebra						
Science Geography	Frye's Adv Geog	Completed	34	5	Very Good	
Elementary Science	Stowells Physiology	Completed				March 27th

(Table continued)

Subject	Text book	Amount	No. of weeks	Periods per week	Rank	Date of Completion
History U.S History	Barne's History	To Johnson's Admn	34	5	Fair	
Civics						
Other Subjects English Bible						
Vocal Music						
Drawing	Praug System	Book #2 Completed	34	2	Good	

Signature of Teacher, Principal or Superintendent: *Elda Stambaugh*

Name of School: *Port Norris Public School*

(Actual Document Replicated)

April 26, 1907

Dear Prof Cutler,

Enclosed find a check for Mr. Sanchamo's tuition (of fifty dollars). Will you kindly send bills for him to me. That is his tuition as I am to pay for him. I do hope he will get on well. He is so greatly needed in Assam, his home, as a missionary and we feel greatly interested in his progress—as he has an interesting history being the son I believe of a chief who was the famous 'head slayers' there. He was brought over here by Rev. and Mrs. Perrine our missionaries to Assam. I know you will do all you can to help him as of course he will feel strange and homesick I presume for a while. He expects to reach you Thurs, May 2nd. He hopes to accompany us with Laus at Northfield this Summer, and I expect to come over often and see Sanchamo and the school working.

Cordially yours,

Sarah C. Ropes
10 Morris Ave
Morristown
New Jersey
April 26th

(Actual Document Replicated)

Mount Hermon, Mass.   May 21, 1907

1. Name: *Sanchamo*

2. Have you a trade or a business by which you have earned money?
   No

   What is it?

3. What proportion of your school expenses are you responsible for
   yourself? *None*

4. Do you purpose graduating from Mount Hermon? *I like to*

5. Do you intend to go to college? *I like to*

6. What profession or occupation do you hope to enter? *Teach my
   people*

PLEASE FILL OUT THIS CARD AND
LEAVE IT AT THE PRINCIPAL'S OFFICE

June 26, 1907

Name of Candidate
Sanchamo

Address
Port Norris NJ

Date of birth
About March 1887

Date of filling out this blank
January 24, 1907

When does he wish to enter?
Beginning Summer Term 1907

What form does he hope to enter?
Left for your decision

Does he apply for the full course?
Not necessarily

If not, how long does he intend to remain?
As long as seems wise

Name and address filling out this blank.
Mrs. R.L. Perrine
Port Norris, NJ

Name and address of parent or guardian.
Rev. S.A Perrine
Port Norris

Please fill out the above blanks.

(Actual Document Replicated)

Port Norris

New Jersey

September 26, 1907

My dear Mr. Cutler

In a recent letter to me, Sanchamo speaks of your interest in him, of having been invited to your home to dinner and talking with Dr. Witter while there. I feel very grateful for all your kindness to him and only hope that his study in your school may be a great blessing to him and all of his people through him.

Year before last his eyes troubled him so that he remained out of school for about two weeks. An Optician in Philadelphia thought he would need to put on glasses but after a new of Osteopathic treatment he was so much better, he decided it was not necessary. He went all of last year to school without any trouble with his eyes. I am always seeing to it that he has a good light and wears a green shade when studying at night. He tells me now that his eyes is hurting very much and that his gas light is not sufficient and that he very frequently has very severe headaches so that he must miss some of his lessons. This discourages him very much for he does not want to miss anything while he has the privilege of being in so good a school. I am sorry I did not know of this before his vacation in August as Mrs. Ropes was then in Northfield and undoubtedly would have done whatever was necessary for him. Is it too much to ask of you that you see if he has a proper light in a good position for his study table and that his eyes be examined by a competent Optician if necessary and the necessary means employed to help him? If Mrs. Ropes does not wish to bear the expense, I will manage it in some way myself.

Trusting this request may not seem too burdensome.

Sincerely yours,

Mrs. Perrine

(Actual Document Replicated)

Mount Hermon, Mass October 4th, 1907

1. Name: *Sanchamo L*
2. Have you a trade or business by which you have earned money? *No*
   What is it?
3. What proportion of your school expense are you responsible for yourself? *Nothing*
4. Do you purpose graduating from Mount Hermon? *I do not know*
5. Do you intend to go to college? *No*
6. What profession or occupation do you hope to enter? *Missionary*

(Actual Document Replicated)

October 7, 1907

Benjamin P. Croft, M.D.
1712 Federal Street
Greenfield, Massachusetts

Regular Office Hours	By Appointment
Nine to One	Afternoons
Mon and Sat Eve, 7 to 9	Sundays and Holidays

Prof H.F. Cutler
Mount Hermon
Massachusetts

Dear Mr. Cutler:

I found the examination of Sanchamo's eyes pretty difficult and was finally obliged to use drops and make a second examination and I then uncovered some near sighted astigmatism which I believe to be at the bottom of his eye pain and headache. I advise the constant wear of glasses and another examination in nine to twelve months. I gave him a pair of smoked lenses to wear until his others are made, which will be on Thursday until which time he should not use his eyes.

Yours truly,

Benjamin P. Croft

(Actual Document Replicated)

October 28, 1907

Port Norris
New Jersey

Prof H.F Cutler
Mount Hermon School
Massachusetts

My dear Professor:

Will you kindly send this bill for examination of Sanchamo's eyes to Mrs. Ropes. She is paying for all of his expenses and will be glad to pay this I am sure.

However, if she should not pay it, then of course we will. We are glad to learn of his continued good progress, and are sure that he is getting with you the best possible for him.

Thanking you for all good offices.

Yours and most sincerely,

S.A. Perrine

(Actual Document Replicated)

Nov 14, 1907

Morristown, NJ

Dear Prof Cutler,

I am enclosing check to you as I did not know anything about Sanchamo having trouble with his eyes. It was Mr. Lau that my sister talked about and his eye difficulty. This of Sanchamo must be an entirely new development, so I send check to you thinking perhaps you may have the two confused as Sanchamo was with us there that day in your office, also Mr. Lau.

With kind regards,

Yours truly

Sarah C. Ropes

If this is for Mr. Lau, my sister will pay it. Please return check.

(Sarah Ropes is the sister of Irene Gardner Ropes who sponsored Sanchamo)

(Actual Document Replicated)

December 31st, 1907

10 Morris Ave
Morristown, New Jersey

Dear Mr. Cutler,

Pardon my troubling such a busy man as you are but I am writing on behalf of a boy from the Naga Hills of Assam who was brought over here for an education to learn to help others and learn to know Christ. He has been in this country with these entrusted missionaries' mid-year and is in the public school and doing very good work but of course he has been up hill work for him.

So I am writing to inquire whether you think it's possible for him to enter Mt Hermon for the Summer term and then go in the Fall. I will be responsible for his tuition of course. I enclose Mr. Perrine's letter to me which will explain more fully about this young man. He is about eighteen or twenty I would say and anxious to learn. His father was that of the chief "head taker" of the tribe a warlike savage people but this fellow has a happy Christian face and I believe God has called him to do a noble work for Him among his people someday. Hoping that this busy year will bring joy and happiness to you and yours.

I remain,

Yours Cordially

Sarah G. Ropes
10 Morris Aveh
Morristown, New Jersey

(Actual Document Replicated)

February 7, 1908

Port Norris New Jersey

Mr. Cutler,

My dear sir. Will you kindly excuse Sanchamo to go to Brattleboro to see an Osteopath there about his eyes. Osteopathic treatment has helped him very much and I hope it will do so again. If proper arrangements can be made, I wish him to take treatments regularly for a time at least.

Respectfully,

R.L. Perrine

Sanchamo tells me he has given up his history on account of his eyes. I was wondering if he better not give up the arithmetic and not try it anymore and try something else in its stead. From what I saw of his work when here on Xmas vacation, I doubt if he will do better on third trial than he did before.

Yours Sincerely,

R.L. Perrine

(Actual Document Replicated)

(This letter is undated)

Dear Sir,

Please excuse me that I have missed my writing class so many times by sickness and by forgetting. But the last week I did not forget it but I had headache that reason I did not go down to get my writing class in the morning. But I never cheat my class any time, sometimes I miss my class in time because I have no watch to find exact hour. One day I forgot to tell you what the Doctor has told me about my eyes. He told me to go down to Greenfield if I do not get much better between 8 weeks.

Yours Sincerely,

Sanchamo Lotha

(Actual Document Replicated)

March 4, 1908

Dear Sir:

I never expect to be in mist of you, because I was a heathen boy as well as my brothers and sisters are living now without knowing God. Isaiah 42:16. But by the love of God has brought me here in mist of you. Therefore, I ask you for forgiveness 2 Corinthian 2:5–11. I do not know how often I have done wrong before my roommate or my fellowmen. But especially with my roommate this term. Only God knows all about my struggling and my thoughts. That which have happened so many times. I also will give all to the Lord. I know you have forgiven me many times, and are doing great work for my people in helping me and my Lord Jesus. I am very sorry that I have not shown you my love as I ought to. But kindly decide and forgive me again for my Lords sake. For God brought me here for great purpose for my people who are living in the darkness without knowing God. Bible says if we confess our sins, He is faithful to forgive our sins from all sins and unrighteousness. I am very sorry that I have failed so many times to do good. I may have strength by your prayer.

Yours cordially,

Sanchamo

(Actual Document Replicated)

June 1, 1908

Dear Sir. Mr. Cutter:

Yes, sir, I am determining to go to school here in the Fall term. I am sure, it is my most opportunity and possibility for me to go to school here, because the Lord has opened my way. I also will ask Mrs. Ropes when she will come to Northfield. I am sure she will pay me for the tuition for the Fall term. I cannot count my plan. My determination is to visit the Lord's day and to do his will. My blessings come from heaven. I receive a letter from Mrs. Ropes last week. So there is no doubt. The Lord will help me all way through.

Your's cordially,

Sanchamo L

(Actual Document Replicated)

July 1, 1908

Dear Sir. Mr. Cutter:

I did not know what news you have heard yesterday morning but one of the students held on my wrist and he tried to wring my arm so I tried to pull my arm from his hands, and he held me fast again, so he and I pulled our hand for a while. But it was not just fun of it at all. So please forgive me about it.

Yours Sincerely,

Sanchamo

(Actual Document Replicated)

July 7, 1908

Dear Sir. Mr. Cutler,

I do not know what kind news you have heard from someone interpretations. I am going to write to you whatever I spoke to my friends. God knows from my deepest heart. And my God's witness is greater than my witness and whatever may be, he knows more me more than I do. I put these words before I tell you anything. But let your speech be yea, yea: Nay, nay and the mouth confession is made unto salvation. Please listen to me I tell you. I am very sorry that I disturb you so often. Yet sometimes I cannot plan make plan myself what it is going on. I could not understand you what you have heard between these two weeks.

On the Fourth of July Mr. Aikin and I went to Northfield to see the games. On the way I told him that someone was going to speak something about my fault in the conference and he asked me who found your fault? I told him that someone found my faults, because I have heard about it before Conference was held. This all I told him. And yesterday morning I went to the tyke about Six O'clock to wash my face, there I saw Mr. Archie was coming from the tyke to his room and he forget the soap which he put it on the table where the things put. And I went in and I saw his little soap was lying on the table. And while I was washing my face, then Mr. Dunham came in after that I went out from the tyke closed and came to my room. And at noon Mr. Archie told me that someone stolen away his soap. So I took off him and he and I went to the tyke and I showed to him the place where the soap was laid. At that time the soap was not there, so he and I came out. Before that someone swept out cleaned the room. Only it as far as I can tell you about.

Dear Sir, whatever will come to me I will leave all this at the feet of Jesus as long as he wants me to live here. He did not bring me here merely, but he expects me to carry his message or the gospel to the heathens. I can't explain you that how many people have not yet heard the gospel of Christ. But then He knows all about the heathenism and He brought me here for His service in the future life. I also will not go away from here until the peace of the Lord has come to me, no matter whatever may be fall to upon me. For He says—He giveth power to the faint, and to him that he hath no might he giveth strength. But they that wait for Jehovah shall renew their strength. I never, never let your hand go so if I wait for him he will strengthen me according to his promise. That reason I also joined in the church.

Yes, sir, it is hard and takes strength to be patient for one to another, but Christ has already suffered for us in all things. So please patient for me a little while the Lord will surely comfort us. Also all things above we are able to make peace through the blood of Christ.

Please forgive me what you have heard.

Yours Sincerely,

Sanchamo

(Actual Document Replicated)

(This letter is undated)

Dear Sir:

Please excuse me that I did not take your advice this morning.
I think I will drop the U.S History and take the 2B Bible,
B Arithmetic and B Grammar so I can study along well. I am very
sorry that I did not take your advice this morning. Please excuse
me whenever I make mistake before you I am so sorry that I had
untrained mother sometime hard for me to be considered as quick
as your people do. And hard for me to be reasoned anything. Pray
for me all times.

Yours Cordially,

Sanchamo

(Actual Document Replicated)

J.P Mills, Esquire, I.C.S.,
Sub Divisional Officer Mokokchung
Naga Hills Assam, India

The Principal
Mt Hermon School,
Mt Hermon,
Mass, USA

Dated Mokokchung: The 2nd February 1920

Sir,

I have the honour to inform you that it appears that Sanchamo Lotha if this district studied in your school when Mr. Henry F. Cutler was Principal, having been brought from here by a member of the American Baptist Mission. I should be much obliged if you would let me have a Certificate declaring that Sanchamo read up to such and such a class and that he was of good moral character. The Certificate is required in connection with an application for employment under Government.

With apologies for troubling you in this matter.

I have the honour to be,

Sir,

Your most obedient servant

Signed (JP Mills)
Sub Divisional Officer,
Mokokchung

(Actual Document Replicated)

J.P. Mills

J.P. Mills was a British gentleman posted in the Naga Hills as the sub divisional officer. He wrote several books documenting the customs and culture of the tribes in the Naga Hills. Some of the books written by him include The Lotha Nagas, The Rengma Nagas, The Sema Nagas, The Angami Nagas, and The Ao Nagas.

Changsu Village
August 28, 1922

Dear Mr. H.F Cutler:

I was so glad to receive Mount Hermon Alumni Quarter. Thank you very much. It is a great grateful to you. I was so sorry to make you know that I have not been writing to you for so long time in account of stamps. Last year I received a personal letter from you, so that I went up to Wokha Station to buy stamps but the Post Master told me that he had no foreign stamps so that I came down without it. Even at that time I failed to answer you. I am living a far away from Mission Compound so that it is a hard for me to get stamps for foreign land. Because there is no specially post office here around for stamps so that is a very hard to write letters to any of friends to foreign land. It takes me three days' march to go to our Mission Compound for foreign stamps. There is no place to find letter box up here among the Naga Villages. Here are most of the Nagas are living without education, because most of them superstition. You please not think that I am not regarding to our old Mount Hermon Boys. I am always thinking about Mount Hermon School, because it has been a great interesting for my life. It is also a great helpful to my soul for the influence of Mount Hermon School. I was so glad to attend there even a short time so I am gladly expressing to you of to Mt. Hermonite.

I received two letters when I was in Kuki expedition after I came back from France I went war for two times. I went to France and once I went to Kuki expedition after I came back from France. I was often crowded with rations of coolies or labors. So that I had no a chance of writing letters to any of my friends.

I am living here Changsu Village instead of living at my Village. I am Pastor and teaching some boys here School. I am glad to receive letters from the Mount Hermon School.

It is my best regards to you all.

I have the honor to be Sir,

Sanchamo Lotha Christian

(Letter written by Sanchamo upon his return
to the Naga Hills from the United States).

(Actual Document Replicated)

Dear Sir,

Please excuse me that I did not take your advice this morning. I think I will drops the U. S. History. And take the 2 B. Bible, B arith and B. Gram. So I can study along well. I am very sorry that I did not take your advice this morning. Please excuse me whenever I make mistake before you. I am so sorry that I had a untrained mother. Sometimes hard for me to be considered. as quick as your people do. And hard for me to be reasoned. anything. Pray for me all times.

Yours Cordially
— Sanchamo

Original letter written by Sanchamo)
(Courtesy Northfield Mount Hermon Archives)

Recommendation letter to Mount Hermon School by Mrs. Rose Ermina
Perrine, wife of Rev. S.A. Perrine (Courtesy of Northfield Mount
Hermon Archives) (Actual Document Replicated)

Letter of recommendation by Ms. Elda
G. Stambaugh, Principal of Port Norris
School. (Courtesy of Northfield
Mount Hermon Archives)

◇◇◇◇◇◇◇◇◇◇

A Tribute

Tribute to our Pastor Shanjamo Jungi

(To be sung with the tune Zayi Zayile)

Eramo Shanjamo/ Potsowna ni ethung-checho
Elder Shanchamo/ You were chosen by Our God Almighty

Naga yolo ovungoji/ Americani niwotokcho
The first among the Nagas/Who studied in America

Yikrachio Eramo/ montso pia ni yikrachiala
Our respected, loving elder/ We thank you and appreciate you

Ena ni nongratoko jiang/ Opvui Potsow myingona
For all the pain and heartaches we caused you/ In the name of Jesus

Nlan esiyele/ Naga sukying mhayitokuka
Forgive us/and bless the Nagas from generations to generations

Nina e kangtsutokala/ Potsow Montso pia longshiala
You make us proud/ We joyfully thank our Heavenly Father

Amotsu Shanjamo jo/ Jumang pankawoena khacho
Our Grandpa Shanjamo/ Who studied overseas

Potsow motsu epungnocho/ Ena Potsow mying thungiala
Who taught us the love of Jesus/ We praise God for you

Potsowoe na ndoktav ka/ Yikrachio e omotsu-o
We will meet in Heaven/ Our most esteemed Grandpa

Lyrics by Jan Ezung Nienu

Engraved
"Moody Bible Institute 1886"

Shanjamo's teapot

Shanjamo's personal belongings
displayed at Yikhum Village

Yikhum Village
(gathering place)

Shanjamo Jungi's resting place
at the gate of Yikhum Village, Nagaland

Shanjamo Jungi wearing a tuxedo with all his medals. Courtesy: Rev. Harold
& Harriet Houston (Missionary to the Lotha Nagas 1947–1953)

Shanjamo wearing a traditional Lotha Naga costume.
(Courtesy of the Houstons)

Shanjamo's favorite songs as documented by Mr. N.L Kinghen

Weeping Will Not Save Me

Weeping will not save me
Tho' my face was bathe in tears,
That could not allay my fear,
Could not wash the sins of years,
Weeping will not save me!

Refrain:
    Jesus wept and died for me,
    Jesus suffered on the trees,
    Jesus waits to make me free,
    He alone can save me!

Working will not save me!
Purest deeds that I can do,
Holiest thoughts and feelings too,
Cannot form my souls anew,
Faith in Christ will save me!

He Will Hold Me Fast

When I fear my faith would fail,
Christ can hold me fast
When the tempter will prevail,
He will hold me fast.

Refrain:
    He will hold me fast
    He will hold me fast
    For my Saviour loves me so,
    He will hold me fast

The Wealth of the World Is Jesus

I was poor as the poorest outcast from the fold,
I sank by the wayside with hunger and cold,
But He bade' me look up, all His riches behold,
O the wealth of the world is Jesus.

Chorus:
> I was poor as the poorest outcast from the fold,
> But He gave me great treasures of silver and gold,
> And a mansion above that will never grow old,
> For the wealth of the world is Jesus.

I was poor as the poorest, I wandered alone,
No dwelling had I, and my pillow a stone,
But I heard someone whisper, "I'll make thee my own,"
Now the peace of my heart is Jesus.

I was poor as the poorest, no riches had I,
But Jesus my Saviour, came down from the sky,
And He went to the cross there to suffer and die,
And my soul was redeemed by Jesus.

◇◇◇◇◇◇◇◇◇◇

References

Anderson, Bengt I. *We Lived in Nagaland,* 1978.

Clark, M.M. *A Corner in India.* Philadelphia: American Baptist Publication Society, 1907.

Day, Richard Ward. *A New England Schoolmaster: The Life of Henry Franklin Cutler.* Bristol, Conn.: The Hildreth Press, Inc., 1950.

Elwin, Verrier. *The Nagas in the Nineteenth Century.* Oxford University Press. 1969.

Ezung, P.E. *Nkolo (Ancient), Nchung (Modern), Kyong Liphong Phisa Yansa.* Dimapur: Sethi Printers, G.S. Road.

Falzini, Mark W. *One Square Mile: A History of Trenton Junction, New Jersey.* iUniverse, Bloomington, IN. 2017

Hamilton, Sally Atwood, Editor. *Lift Thine Eyes: The Landscape, the Buildings, the Heritage of Northfield Mount Hermon School.* Mount Hermon, Massachusetts: Northfield Mount Hermon Publisher, 2010.

Houston, Howard and Harriet. *Nagaland Adventure 1947–1953.* Dimapur, Nagaland: Mahibir Printing Press, G.S. Road.

Kinghen, N. L. *A Brief Life Sketch of Shanchamo Lomongo Lotha.* Wokha, 1972. Kohima Printing Press.

Mills, J.P. *The Lhota Nagas.* London: Macmillan and Co, Limited, 1922.

Murry, Ezamo. *Thus Saith the Missionaries: A Collection of Valuable Records of the Early Missionaries on the Naga Church in General and the Kyong Lotha in Particular*, 1979.

Nagaland Baptist Church Council, 2012.

Nienu. V. *Naga Cultural Milieu*. San Francisco: Dorylus Publishing Group, 2015.

Okotso Baptist Ekhumkho Motsu. 1904–2004. Centennial Jubilee Celebration

Pollock, John. *Billy Graham, Evangelist to the World: An Authorized Biography of the Decisive Years*. San Francisco: Harper and Row Publishers, 1979.

Takam, S. *Imlomg Chang: A Biography*, 1999.

Yikhum Baptist Ekhunkho Motsu: Nzyu 1898–1998. Dimapur, Nagaland: New Printing Press, Church Road.

◇◇◇◇◇◇◇◇◇◇◇

About the Author

D R. JAN EZUNG NIENU currently serves as the executive director
of a large child care center in Northern California. She has served
as an adjunct faculty member at the Golden Gate Baptist Theo-
logical Seminary in Mill Valley and at Patten University in Oakland
as the chair of the early childhood studies. She received her doctorate
from the University of San Francisco, California. Jan also served as the
corps advisor of education in Alameda County and continues to serve
as a professional growth advisor to the early childhood professionals.
She mentors and provides support to teachers and directors in the
field of early childhood studies in the Bay Area, San Francisco. She is
originally from Nagaland, northeast of India.

She is wearing a Lotha Naga shawl in honor of Shanjamo Jungi,
as she is also from the Lotha Naga Tribe. She is the first lady from the
Lotha Naga Tribe to receive a doctoral degree.

June 10, 2019

In the 1840s, the Rev. Miles Bronson and his wife entered the Naga Hills, but their ministry was halted due to an illness. They were followed by Dr. Clark and his wife Mary Mead Clark in 1872. American Baptist missionaries were the first to come to the Naga Hills to teach the gospel of Jesus Christ.

American Baptist missionaries were and still are amazing Christians in their devotion to bringing the gospel to people throughout the world. The story of how the headhunters of the Naga Hills in the Northeast of India became Christians is one that merits reading because we learn how much God wants all people to come to know Jesus as their personal Lord and Savior.

I can't even imagine walking through fields where heads of people had been cut off. What faith and trust in God those missionaries had to have had to even be willing to go into those areas of the world.

I am the beneficiary of how God changed those hearts because Dr. Jan Ezung Nienu is one of my very best friends. She is an amazing woman of faith who has helped so many young children and families in the San Francisco Bay Area and beyond to come to know Christ.

I was privileged to work with her on the preschool and kindergarten committee for many years in the First Baptist Church of Richmond, California. I know she will continue to enrich the lives of a new generation of children throughout the world. God bless Dr. Jan Ezung Nienu.

Joanne Pike
Retired Registrar/Admissions Director
American Baptist Seminary of the West
Berkeley, California

The famous evangelist D. L. Moody once said, "The world has yet to see what God will do with a man fully consecrated to Him." Born in the last decade of Mr. Moody's life, Shanjamo Jungi was a man whose consecrated life God used to play a major role in the transformation of his world—Nagaland, the nation of his birth. After being educated in the United States at the school founded by D.L. Moody, Shanjamo returned to the then Naga Hills to share the gospel of Christ with the people he loved.

Author Jan Ezung Nienu, a Naga native, writes with a heart of gratitude for not only Shanjamo, but also the early missionaries who left their own country to share the gospel with the headhunting Nagas. Readers will enjoy a fascinating journey filled with firsthand accounts, family interviews, original correspondence, and regional photographs that tell the story of the impact of Christianity on a nation. When speaking of the influence of Christianity, one Naga pioneer Mr. Imlong Chang explained, "…our people have been greatly blessed by the coming of Christianity. How good it is that it is now possible for the head and the body to be buried together."

Made in the USA
San Bernardino, CA
18 June 2020

73719468R00082